*When I was eleven, I died and went to Heaven,*
*And this is what I saw:*


I could not breathe.
I knew that I was drowning.
I knew that I was powerless and would cease to be
And a panic overtook me.

Helpless to escape,
I surrendered to the inevitable
And was pulled from my body
Pulled through the darkness
To the very RIM of Being.
There I remained suspended
Sucked into the Cosmic Void
Where two scintillating, singing dancing bolts of lightning
Joyously entwined me in their embrace.

"Who Are You?" I asked,
And they answered, "We Are You."

And I KNEW that was so.
And I felt all the WARMTH of Their LOVE.
And I remembered that I had been there before
In a place SO FAMILIAR.
And I knew that I had come HOME
Home to the very GROUND of My Being.
I was content to remain there
Scintillating, singing, dancing with them
And all my FEAR was gone.


*Then I was rescued and pulled back to this world*
*Retching and against my will.*

*Since that time, I no longer fear Death.*


*Artemis Smith* 2015

CONTENTS

a Monograph of
THE SAVANT GARDE INSTITUTE

"ArtemisSmith's ATHEIST MANIFESTO" by Annselm L.N.V. Morpurgo, M.A., CPC
© 2015 by The Savant Garde Institute. All rights reserved.

Academic Library Edition: ISBN 978-1-878998-28-6
LIBRARY OF CONGRESS CONTROL NO: 2015909404

'the savant garde workshop' publishers
P.O.B. 1650 . SAG HARBOR . NEW YORK . 11963 . USA
Tel: 1.631.725.1414

ArtemisSmith's

# ATHEIST MANIFESTO

## A Unified Scientist's Creed

by Annselm L.N.V. Morpurgo

the
savant garde workshop ™
Sag Harbor . New York . U.S.A.

Annselm L.N.V. Morpurgo is a futurist poet and scientific philosopher. She is also known and published in the arts as ArtemisSmith, founder and stylizer of the Unisex and Unirace Movements. Also as a cult figure and strategist of the early Rainbow rights coalitions, she was the first invited speaker to tell the Gay Community to hurry up and "Come out of the Closet!" or get left out of the civil rights putsch. In 1965 this caused a deep divide inside the movement. Many felt it was too soon and that ArtemisSmith had to be shunned or otherwise silenced.

In 1966, a suspicious car accident left ArtemisSmith seriously injured. She chose, during her long period of recuperation, to complete her scientific education and immersed herself in doctoral studies under a full-tuition scholarship awarded her at The City University of New York. Coincidentally, many of the East Coast deeply closeted leaders of the pre-Stonewall Gay movement were by then also concentrated at C.U.N.Y., some as Faculty and some as academic-military-industrial-complex activist infiltrators within the CIA, NSA, and FBI who had subsequently fallen into the grip of organized crime and had been made unwilling slaves of the corrupt establishment.


In 1972, even while presenting her ground-breaking papers on neurophilosophy at key information science conferences, Annselm L.N.V. Morpurgo was suddenly dropped without cause from both the Adjunct Faculty and the C.U.N.Y. Doctoral Program in Philosophy, despite having strong academic support for her dissertation and having completed nearly every Department requirement toward the Ph.D. The investigator from the American Philosophical Association's Committee on the Status of Women eventually concluded that the underlying cause appeared to be "political."

The papers Annselm L.N.V. Morpurgo had presented to the scientific community, explicating the New Concept of Mind under Information Science, eventually resulted in the 1981 award of a well-earned Nobel Prize to Split-Brain Researcher R.W. Sperry. But still missing was the Logical characterization dispelling any 'ghost-in-the-machine" presented since 1970 and published in retrospect herein.

*The liberation of Humanity from the tyranny of false religious ideologies must center on a clarification of the Nature of Mind and the underlying universal Architecture of the Human Form.*

*From the Artist's standpoint, as cultural master-builder, such a project must be both Scientific and Political.*

*Toward that end, presented here are ArtemisSmith's futurist papers explicating the revised concepts of Gender and Species under 21ˢᵗ Century Unified Science.*

Such an investigation into the New Concept of Mind requires parallel thinking toward a synoptic *Godel Convergence*.

The history of that creative peripathetic is set down here and it is strongly recommended that this collection of *Notes* be read at tandem with the 2013 larger Poetic Anthology by the same Author:

978-1-878998-20-0  376 pp.
*"ArtemisSmith's* GrandmaMoseX
*The Final Testament before The Apocalypse"*

# ArtemisSmith's *Thus Spake* GrandmaMoseX

## The Final Testament before The Apocalypse

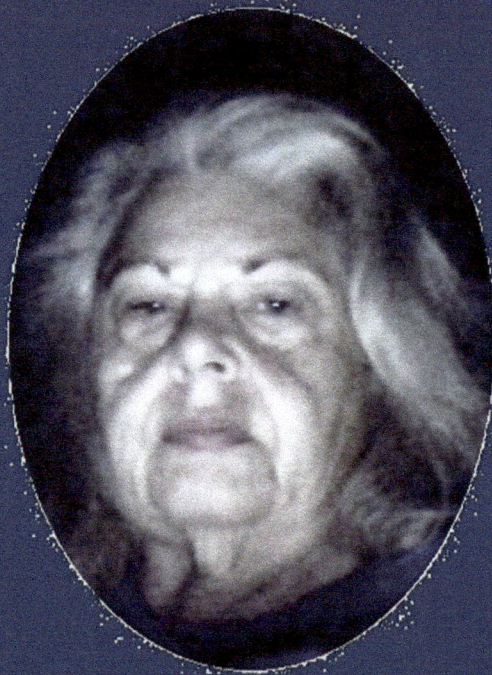

By Annselm L.N.V. Morpurgo

*the* savant garde workshop
SAG HARBOR . NEW YORK . USA

# 1. Can Atheism Become a Genuine Religion?

Is the term *God* as ontologically trivial as the term *Phlogiston*?

I remember that the first time this question came up in a really serious way was when my artistic life-partner and mentor, Billie Ann Taulman, first shaved the remnants of my adolescent stubble with Occam's Razor. Fortunately, neither of us had yet been corrupted by the language analyst's need for logical precision - a sophistication that would have thoroughly apoplexied our budding artistic thought. Our naive approach was purely intuitive, commonsensical. Taulman was describing the fundamental tenets of her native Methodism; I, as an offspring of Freemason Scientific Unitarians.

Our initial question, posed as artists and poets, was:

How are we to picture |God|?
> do we use the Methodist equation, |God=Love|,
> or the Einsteinian one, |God=Absolute Truth|?

Taulman cut through the confusion with one of her sweeping *Gestaldt* shifts:

> why contemplate |God| at all?
> why not simply contemplate |Love=Absolute Truth|?

Suddenly both of us stopped and held our breath - yes, such an equation embodied genuine pictorial simplicity, one rooted in Human genetico-moral intuition - an aesthetic equation that allowed a higher level language icon to replace all heretofore godhead idolatries:

$$|Love=AbsoluteTruth=TheBeautiful|=|TheSacred|$$

Our artistic purpose spontaneously blended into one voice - now we knew the direction in which each of us would proceed. Together we would masterbuild a whole new metaphysic, a scientifically-based "small-c" catholicism, one better suited to the universally ꟷTrueꟷ concept of Human Identity - one that would finally succeed in sweeping all the merchants of falsehood and idolatry from the one and only universally accepted mystical intuition, wherein the notion of ꟷScientific Truthꟷ might be held synonymous with ꟷThe Sacredꟷ!

This artistic vision marked the beginning of our mutual, 'Mystical-Atheism.'

We paused to examine our new protocol:

> [Mystical-Atheism], an oxymoron?
> No!
>
> But isn't the Atheist's position that nothing need be held ꟷSacredꟷ ultimately logically self-contradictory?
> Yes!
>
> But then, is it logically possible for an Atheist to hold anything ꟷSacredꟷ and still be an Atheist?
>
> Again, Yes! despite all Grand Inquisitors' best efforts to suppress this logico-political possibility.

To understand how this is possible, one must begin by dismissing all religious zealots who set up verbal pseudoconstructs regarding the psychological nature of skepticism.

There are at least two kinds of atheistic positions, only one of which is logically untenable:

> 1. Atheist=nontheist/nonidolatrist, someone who may at least minimally believe in ꟷTruthꟷ (i.e., whether it be aesthetic or scientific or merely logicotheoretical truth) but not in any deity.
>
> 2. Atheist=nihilist, someone who believes in nothing, not even logic, or any belief whatsoever including their own atheism.

8

The latter definition, reflecting the straw-man position most often opportunistically attacked by the ardent theist, most certainly belongs to a schizophrenic fool trapped in paradox.

But not so the former, which can point to any number of perfectly sane and intelligent persons (including but not restricted to Buddhists and Ethical Culturists) who are capable of leading a value-laden life filled with Humanist ideals and commitments, normal relationships, ambitions, things believed to be at least existentially |True| and aesthetically |Beloved, Valued, Preserved|, and therefore deeply held existentially |Sacred|.

The confusion regarding Atheism-1 arises when the religious zealot falsely equates the first definition with Agnosticism in order to avoid widespread social conflict and allow peaceful multinational diplomatico-religio-political co-existence.

Unlike Atheist-1, the more socially acceptable Agnostic has no religious commitment, no religious affiliation.

Atheist-1, on the other hand, perilously and religiously denies the existence of any deity - Atheism-1 therefore reflects a fully defined, in no way politically-neutral, fully-committed religious creed of its own which, howbeit politically counter to other creeds, may Constitutionally and legitimately subscribe to a firm set of existential |Truths| and personal objects held |Sacred| within some Nation holding to a sufficient |separation of Church and State| that will tolerate this degree of religious freedom.

But why might anyone perversely choose any form of Atheism over the more socially acceptable fence-sitting alternative of Agnosticism, which can exist under any political regime?

The answer is definitely moral - as well as epistemological:

Agnosticism allows a much larger ontology - all the gods and all the mythologies of all the various religions, not just some of them.

The logically-consistent Agnostic, though perhaps not drowning in paradox like the nihilistic Atheist-2, is doomed to drown in the polluted sea of tolerance *for even the most bizarre elements of religious extremism,* including genocide, human sacrifice, and sexual slavery.

The Atheist-1, in contrast, by dismissing all gods as excessive and epistemologically intrusive, achieves a purist environment of informational clarity - one that can be guided solely by genetico-moral intuition wherein true Human goals and strategies are more easily identified.

In 1955, bringing the whole world toward a religiously committed Atheism-1 thus became our artistic manifesto. The political story of our activist partnership is chronicled in a volume published in 2011: *"ArtemisSmith's* ODD GIRL Revisited: an autobiographical correlate."  This essay on Mystical Atheism stands at tangent to it.

Recent statements by many prominent persons including cosmologist Stephen Hawking regarding the lack of necessity in belief in any deity with respect to the search for Absolute Truth through the physical sciences has sparked an immediate need to remind the scientific community that generations of other philosophers as well as a couple of modern poets and political activists said it first more than fifty-five years ago!

Taulman remains among the most brilliant and original thinkers with whom I have been fortunate to intimately interface, although scarcely any of her poetry was ever finished. It does not matter if she finished what she started, it nevertheless sparked new visions in me, and if I have stolen her soul in any or many of my works, it is not because I mean to take the credit for myself - but rather that we are so generically entwined in our thoughts that there is no possibility of separating us.  In the attempt to capture only a small spark of her magnificent mind I have interspersed some of her rescued visions in these pages.

Back in the winter of 1954-55 when we first began our dialogue, Taulman and I already realized that |Human Beings| were on the verge of changing form.

(Amusingly, both of us admitted that we already pictured ourselves as sprouting new wings on our back - as budding Angels, or more naturalistically, re-evolving Pterodactyls - wherefore my first collection of poems, *Hark the Pterodactyl,* pointed to that vision.)

In 1955, even as radical as we were, our concept of Human Identity seemed nevertheless clearly defined and fixed. Nevermind that our original equation |Love = Truth| made neither logical nor mathematical nor Boolean sense. It did make |Common Sense|.

We knew what |Love| entails - that biofeeling that comes naturally and spontaneously to genetico-morally intact |Human| beings to care for something or someone in a nurturing way.

And we knew what |Truth| involves - a consensus of opinions among sane and educated persons within a scientific community sharing in a common epistemology.

Therefore, at that time our original equation |Love=Truth|=|The Sacred| seemed entirely unproblematic. All we had to do was preserve the economic-political-cultural conditions that nurture |Human| development.

By 1958 however, when I first began *The SKEETS Triptych*, it became clear to me that |Human Identity| is immensely fragile and so thoroughly relative that

|Human Common Sense as dictated by Private Conscience|=
|The Moral|=|The Sacred|

can and does often fade from view even in the best of econo-politico-cultural environments. Why then, I asked myself, do I continue to defend my Mystical-Atheism as the only tenable creed?

I could not answer my own question until I had finished the second book of *SKEETS* and started putting everything together into my initial papers on the explanation and simulation of Human Consciousness.

By then, having had sufficient time to reflect on all the scientific discoveries now making themselves fully felt at the turn of this century, I came to realize that a subtle change in the new economies of *Human Potential* does indeed threaten *all* genetico-moral concepts of |The Self|.

In the information explosion and its exponential increase in the speed of intercultural communication there is now for many a real danger of loss of identity as a Species altogether, unless we declare a new higher level equation:

**The Sacred = Private Conscience as shaped by the Laws of the Unified Sciences**

But how retrograde Socratic! Are we secretly reintroducing "The Gods" in our dialogue? *Which* Laws? *Which* Sciences?

Again recall Occam's principle of parsimony: what need have we for more than existential |Truth| and values we hold |Sacred| to guide us? Let us not multiply entities!

But now that we are multiplying genetic possibilities, and with them, new forms of genetico-moral intuitions, forcing us to contemplate more realistically the possibility of having to politically coexist not only with Psychopaths and Degenerates who look exactly like us but have no |Human Common Sense|, but also with Dolphins, Chimpanzees, Androids and genetically-altered Clones - and even Ourselves genetically-improved, now soon virtually immortal, physically perfect in our "beauty", all of us wealthy, "happy" and nearly indestructible - where does the equation |Common Sense=Human Intuition| take us?

Traditionally, our |Humanity| was preserved through one or another religious creed, though notoriously not all creeds can agree on common |Human| values. And there's the rub!

The rise of powerful rival religions has no more provided us with an amalgam of |Humanist| thought than has the rise of conflicting political parties caused us to unite in |Humanistic| ideologies.

In fact, Religion and Political Ideology go hand in hand, and it is only in countries that separate Church from State that Individual Conscience has been given any substantial room to move.

Banning Religion altogether as subversive of the enlightened State does nothing to solve the real problem for it is unrealistic to maintain that any Nation can exist without Religion anymore than it can exist in abject Anarchy.

Religion is what |Human Identity| is all about. Without it, we lose whatever part of our |Humanity| the political system allows us to preserve. Without it, we fail to nurture the young to moral maturity. Without it we lose all sense of Community and without a |Love for The Sacred| we lose sight of all reason for Being.

But to say all this is not to say we need any specific "God" to complete the picture. It suffices for us to worship |Truth| as a goal of reason, and to hold that for |Truth| to be genuine and relatively stable, it must be existentially grounded in an {Other}={a body of empirical evidence preserved by a community committed to a scientifically organized body of knowledge} that gives rise and force to an *ethic of inclusion* based upon ever evolving and self-correcting |Common Sense|.

But "God" as an ontological posit has become both politically and epistemically cumbersome, posing an increasingly strong argument for holding that it carries no greater explanatory force than the vestigial adherence to "Phlogiston" as a causal entity within the modern theory of combustion.

There are of course persons who will continue to argue that postulating the existence of "God" as a causal entity, even though vestigial, is harmless, even psychologically beneficial, based entirely on faith since no logical or physical form of proof can be presented in its defense.

Then *why not* hold on to God as an aesthetic and reassuring posit to help children sleep soundly and for the dying to desperately invoke?

To such feeble arguments the Mystical Atheist must adopt a polemic stance: *The posit of a deity is neither harmless nor aesthetically nor psychologically reassuring.*

It leads to self-deception and often dangerous behavior and ultimately denies IThe Selfl the opportunity for full moral development.

While phenomenological introspection reveals a number of voices of IThe Selfl, Private Conscience is never to be mistaken for IThe Voice of Godl if madness is to be averted; nor is there any comfort more immediate than the companionship of IPrivate Consciencel even unto death.

Why live a precarious lie, and why die embracing one? Better to die embracing IThe Selfl and its ILove of Othersl as the most worthwhile of objects - for that entity does have an eternal INamel and an immediate IFacel.

Moreover, *Pascal's Choice* be trashed, if by the remotest of chances there really were some *omnipotent, all-knowing, benevolent supreme being* out there peering into our innermost ISelfl, wouldn't such a confrontation with the *Goodness* inherent in one's own Private Conscience also suffice to grant an entry into *that* "Heaven"?

This then, in my eighth decade of reflection, remains my full-flung Religion and I continue to stand as a fully committed Mystical Atheist.

I defend the need for all enlightened communities to convert to my creed - for I see this as the only epistemologically tenable stance equal to the task of truly preserving IHuman Identityl through an increasingly progressive evolutionary change.

The world is becoming much too small to allow for arcane thought and no other creed can offer a more compelling reason to obey the rules of reason and sanity, as dictated both by science and genetico-moral sensibility.

**I do now know IMy Namel but what shall be IMy Facel?**

The aesthetic problem, for the artist/philosopher converted to Mystical Atheism, remains the same:

how do we preserve Beauty in the Human subject?

Isn't all observation grounded in the Observer? And if the Observer is traveling in time and constantly shifting in its parameters, who is to say what

|Love|, |Truth|, |Beauty|, |Common Sense| are? Without a grounding in a |Particular Person|, i.e., an Absolute god-image, will there not be a danger in the loss of |True Human Identity|?

If we must create such a relativistic locally-defined 'graven image', which even Scripture holds "Abominable," to satisfy our animal craving to engage in "worship" of whatever inner voice appears to us as proceeding from the dictates of "Private Conscience," let us not confuse it with any metaphysical posit of what truly may constitute an |extra-linguistic and hence nonsensical| characterization| of |The Sacred|.

This epistemologically polemic stance may not be as satisfying as we would like it to be, but we are stuck with it nevertheless, for there can be no grounding in what gibberish lies entirely beyond language or meta-language or meta-meta-language.

But this does not mean we ought to dispense with all Religion.

Religion is part of our |Human| nature. Our instincts as social animals cannot be ignored. The need for religio-political thought and positive community action is written in our genes.

Though its source remains unnamed, its zealous practice should be open to all, even to the Mystical Atheist. Nations and Temples, being *one and the same thing* in most socio-historical contexts, require a body of beliefs about *Truth, Justice, Fairness, etc.*, written into their laws and customs.

Often, there are minorities whose own persuasions conflict but are allowed to co-habit in peace because obedient to their laws.

As a member of a genuine religion, the Mystical Atheist must also stand among them and seek to peacefully persuade and evangelize as all the others do. There is no problem therefore in the Mystical Atheist's formulation of a special creed and the erection of proper temples in which its own form of community action and education may take place.

But what shall a temple to the scientific ideal of |Humanistic Truth=The Sacred| contain and include? Certainly *not* Scientology or any other pseudo-scientific concoction, either Asian or Western.

Minimally, the religio-political position of the Mystical Atheist *must be* one of pious obedience to "Private Conscience" as shaped by a scientifically-enlightened body of law, and to hold spiritual allegiance solely to a scientifico-moral, relativistic and purely local characterization of |Humanistic Truth=The Sacred| and *not to posit or believe in any untenable extra-linguistic* Absolute

14

Entity.

Restated more practically, it should be housed within a system of universal public education from childhood to the grave that promotes loving relationships and critical thinking - coupled with constant civic vigilance and a stable political climate - one committed to a strict separation of Church and State within an open society and an electoral climate that preserves peaceful dissent and nurtures ‖Private Conscience‖.

*Artemis Smith* 1972

Billie Taulman with Self-Portrait, 1954.

Billie Ann Taulman-Morpurgo  1929 – 2008
On the porch of our federalist townhouse in Sag Harbor 1999

# 2. Irrational Mental Models

(This two-part lecture was presented by ArtemisSmith at various New York City locations including Hunter College, Ligoa Duncan Galerie des Arts, The Community Church of New York, and The Café Rienzi in the Period 1960-1966.

In its expanded form, it was also presented to Professor Peter Caws at Hunter College's Department of Philosophy as part of Annselm L.N.V. Morpurgo's scholarship application to The City University of New York's Doctoral Program.)

PART I: (Language Analysis)

(a) the word-token as phenomenon
(b) contextual transmutation
(c) meaning-blindness

**C.D. Broad** [C.D. Broad, "The Traditional Problem of Body and Mind," *Classics of Analytic Philosophy,* R.R. Ammerman, Ed., McGraw-Hill New York:1965 (85-107)] **discusses the traditional problem of whether any one-one correlation exists between events in a mind and events in the brain and nervous system of the body which it animates. He concludes that since there is no empirical evidence at all for a parallelism of events between mind and brain, if the doctrine is to be held, the grounds for it must be general.**

**While his essay was written in 1925 and much more is now known about psycho-neural parallelism of events, it does contain some important observations. The one that concerns us here is the clear distinction he draws between the mental processes that accompany voluntary action and those associated with reflex actions.**

"...really, the mind and its actions are not literally in Space at all, and the time which is occupied by the mental event is no doubt *also* occupied by some part of the physiological process...There is a clear introspective difference between the mental accompaniment of voluntary action and that of reflex action...The really important difference is that, in the deliberate action, the response is varied *appro-*

"There are mice on the moon ?" and other Sacred Relics

# *Layouts for a Modern Palazzo*

Revelations
from
The
Magnificent
Mind
of
Rainbow
Martyr

## B. Taulman

wrongly
diagnosed
and
institutionalized
on
Ward's
Island
from
1962
to
1966

Drawing by Billie Taulman   c. 1988

THE SAVANT GARDE INSTITUTE

the
savant garde workshop

Sag Harbor . New York . U.S.A.

★ *Poster Exhibit and Reading by ArtemisSmith* ★

New York Public Library at

# Jefferson Market

Wednesday 5 June 2013
6pm to 8pm

425 Avenue of the Americas (at 10th Street)

*priately* to meet the special circumstances which are supposed to exist at the time or are expected to arise later; whilst reflex action is not varied in this way, but is blind and almost mechanical.

"...what the mind does to the body in voluntary action, it it does anything, is to lower the resistance of certain synapses and to raise that of others. The result is that the nervous current follows such a course as to produce the particular movement which the mind judges to be appropriate at the time...In pure reflexes the mind cannot voluntarily affect the resistance of the synapses concerned, and so the action takes place in spite of it. In habitual action it deliberately refrains from interfering with the resistance of the synapses, and so the action goes on like a complicated reflex."

The classical question of mind-body interaction dates earlier than Hume, so that it is surprising that so many philosophers have pursued what seems to me an irrelevant side-issue in the ontological question of whether brain states and mind states coincide. The question is not whether a one-one correspondence exists but rather, how qualitatively efficient is the model, in its entirety, in the portrayal of the separate parts of the original? Isn't there a *Gestalt* difference?

Wittgenstein drew a distinction between copies that merely follow a one-one correspondence with the original, and copies that bear a similarity to the original.

"Roughly speaking, copies are good pictures when they can be easily mistaken for what they represent. A plane projection of one hemisphere of our terrestrial globe is not a picture by similarity or a copy in this sense. It would be conceivable that I portrayed someone's face by projecting it in some queer way, though correctly according to the adopted rule of projection, on a piece of paper, in such a way that no one would normally call the projection 'a good portrait of so and so' because it would not look a bit like him." [L. Wittgenstein, The Blue and Brown Books," Harper & Row. New York:1960 (37)]

Seen in this light, one might propose that some mental models of brain states are more efficient than others - and this would also dissolve the question of solipsism as relevant to our common knowledge of the outside world, since a solipsistic interpretation of reality would depend, not upon the efficiency of the individual model, but upon the subject's falling into a 'normal' range of interpretation of reality, whether or not the 'normal' range encompassed the individuals possessing the most efficient models (e.g., both heightened perception and lowered perception are regarded as abnormal conditions).

The problem of determining what constitutes an efficient mental model of a brain state will be explored in this two-part paper. Part I will be primarily concerned with the word-token treated as phenomenon rather than as sign, and a discussion of the term "meaning-blindness" as it exists in psychopathology as opposed to its use by the language analysts.

The word-token as phenomenon is known to contain at least the following psychophysical characteristics: [The following enumeration is not derived from any one source but as a result of my digestion of numerous discussions on the word-token, primarily by Freud, Jung, Fenichel, McLuhan and Zipf.]

1. (Auditory) its psycho-biological phonemic range, outside of which a spoken word is unrecognizable/unintelligible.

2. (Visual) its inner psycho-biological structure which, besides the juxtaposition of vowels and consonants and the common prefixes and suffixes which may be termed its atomic parts, manifests itself (a) as the containment of unrelated other word-tokens [e.g. the written and spoken English word *smother* contains the word *mother, other, the, her,* and an incomplete *there, here,* etc.] and (b) its typography, which evokes different associations depending upon whether the word-token is handwritten, typewritten, etc

3. (Audio-visual-tactile and/or poetic) its rhyme, off-rhyme, meter, accent, length and associational content/quality.

4. (Signal function) its capabilities, in some individuals, to set off a psycho-biological set/series of responses such as a conditioned reflex; also, its ideogrammic or iconic significance such as is found in magical incantations.

From my clinical observations as aesthetic researcher of schizophrenic language patterns done over a period of years under psychiatric guidance in an effort to determine the poetic element present in the language of the unconscious, I am led to the conclusion that a good deal of irrational language originates from an intermingling of the two roles of the word-token: its intellectual use as symbol, and its psycho-biological function as direct phenomenon.

This irrationality need not be pathological - indeed, the best examples of this intermingling occur in artistic works. The pathological component seems to be the involutional resort to such speaking and thinking patterns.

Perhaps a general discussion of typical schizophrenic modes of communication might prove useful here. Not all of these characteristics bear a direct relationship to the dual use of the word-token but they do reveal some of the many multilinear forms that language can assume other than the co-called normal or rational (unilinear logic).

The following are paraphrased excerpts from Kasanin's landmark analysis: [J.S. Kasanin, "Language and Thought in Schizophrenia," Univ. of California Berkeley:1946 (119-121)]

"Contrary to so-called normal thinking which confines itself to a unitary field - that is - a single realm or frame of reference, the thinking of the schizophrenic is characterized by a frequent and unconscious change of *set*. It is as if he has reverted to a prelogical stage of childhood and the over-generalization of objects that share a far-fetched similarity. In place of well-knit sequences, he appears unable to do more than throw together a cluster of more or less related elements. One patient, for example, when asked what caused the wind to blow, said it was "due to velocity, due to loss of air, evaporation of water…the contact of trees, of air in the trees." Another completed the sentence - "I get warm when I run because …" with the couplet:

> "Quickness, blood, heart of deer, length,
> Driven power, motorized cylinder, strength."

Ferenczi observes that the child, like the adult unconscious, identifies objects on the basis of their slightest resemblance (I.e., everything that opens is a door), "displacing affects with ease from one to another and giving the same name to all. Such a name is thus the highly condensed representative of a large number of fundamentally different individual things which, however, are in some way or other, even if ever so distantly, similar and are for this reason identified." [R. Marshall, unpublished notes for Master's thesis, Hunter College Psychology Dept., New York City; paraphrased from S. Ferenczi, "Sex in Psychoanalysis." (276)]

The absence of the unitary field phenomenon has often been confused with another language deviation, that of the "word salad" which need not have pathological origin. This and the "neologism" when used in connection with schizophrenia are termed forms of asyndetic communication, appearing as autistic - that is - as a sign of withdrawal and lack of concern for the listener, or as an incongruent (ambiguous) reply. [For a discussion of normal patterns of variegation in the maintaining of equilibrium between over-articulation and under-articulation in speech, see Zipf, *Supra*, (212-224)]

Both the "word salad" and the neologism are old-time poetic devices and also one of the ways that language evolves through time. One need only point to Joyce's *Finnegan's Wake* or the works of Gertrude Stein. Especially the hypnotic quality present in Stein's obscure, seemingly nonsensical phrases can be attributed to her dual use of the word-token both as sign and phenomenon. For example, the following passage which sounds differently to the ear than it reads to the eye:

> "With be there all their all their time there
> be there fine there be vine time there be there
> time there all their time there."

By use of the off-rhyme Stein exchanges *with* for *would, be vine* for *divine* and *be mine; their* and *there* are used interchangeably. When this passage is read aloud, it resembles the ringing of bells; it is from the Procession in her "Four Saints in Three Acts" and is a hymn about the after-life which, to the saints, promises a blissful and loving state of being.

Haley discusses ambiguity in schizophrenic communication, pointing out that it is a form of evasion: [J. Haley, "An Interactional Description of Schizophrenia," *Psychiatry 22* 1959 (321-332)]

> "By qualifying his messages to other people incongruently, the schizophrenic avoids indicating what behavior is to take place in his relationships...Preliminary investigations of schizophrenic patients interacting with their families suggest that the patient's way of qualifying his statements incongruently is a habitual response to incongruent messages from his parents...A person can avoid defining his relationship by negating any or all of these four elements:
>
> 1. He can deny that it was *he* who communicated something by saying that someone else said or by assuming an alias, or saying that God spoke to him.
> 2. He can deny that something was communicated, by manifesting amnesia or by making up a new language which cannot be understood and then claiming that has been misunderstood, or, by treating words not as instruments of communication but as things in themselves.
> 3. He can deny that it was communicated to the other person, i.e., to an invisible third party or said to himself, or by addressing the other person's status position rather than to him personally.
> 4. He can deny the context in which it was communicated, perhaps labeling his statements as referring to some other time or place: i.e., "I used to be treated badly in the future." Such a temporal qualification denies he is being treated badly in the present.

To the above, I would like to add that in my own observations, these forms of evasion were not always automatically employed by the patients - i.e., did not seem to be merely reversions to some primitive state or childhood stage but were in fact highly intellectual responses to absurd questions and situations. It sometimes seemed that the contextual meaning of both the answer and the question involved the total environment as part of the sentence, in a heightened perception sense, which bring to mind an observation by Wittgenstein:

> "One expression is no more direct than the other. The meaning of the expression depends entirely on how we go on using it. Let's not imagine the meaning as an occult connection the mind makes between a word and a thing, and that this connection *contains* the whole usage of a word as the seed might be said to contain the tree." [Wittgenstein op. cit.(73-74)]

## Other sections of his *Blue Book* are also pertinent here:

> "Imagine a language in which, instead of 'I found nobody in the room,' one said "I found Mr. Nobody in the room.' Imagine the philosophical problems that would arise out of such a convention." (W 69);

## and, what also might be analogous of some schizophrenic language activity:

> "…we find that there is puzzlement and mental discomfort, not only when our curiosity about certain facts is not satisfied or when we can't find a law of nature fitting in with al our experience, but also when a notation dissatisfies us - perhaps because of various associations which it calls up. Our ordinary language, which of all possible notations is the one which pervades all our life, holds our mind rigidly in one position…and in this position sometimes it feels cramped, having a desire for other positions as well…Our mental cramp is loosened when we are shown the notations which fulfil these needs." (W 59)

To this I might add the tantalizing question of what sort of schizophrenic language deviation might be found in a language that was in itself ambiguous? Would a Hopi schizophrenic deviate into English idiom?

Probably not, because of other factors involved. However, it's reasonable to suspect that mild schizophrenia goes unnoticed among primitive tribes because the nature of the language does not reveal the deviant viewpoint. And in like manner, the inaccuracy in our own language permits many unclear thinkers to sound reasonably coherent.

It seems that we have now made the transition from a discussion of the word-token as phenomenon to the new "sign meaning" it acquires when taken in the context of normal communication through language. The examination of its contextual transmutation will lead us to a clearer understanding of the term "meaning-blindness."

Let us imagine a language composed entirely of objects rather than words, set apart from the natural environment by the addition of a human manipulator who arranges the relation of objects in a structured or teleological order.

Such a language exists among infants who communicate by gestures and sounds rather than words; it also exists in the experimental sciences whenever nature is explored and translated in its own (physical) terms (i.e., such as when a reading on a barometer takes the place of the air pressure it represents).

Such a substitution also occurs in certain types of poetry, and here perhaps can be found our best examples of contextual transmutation. Take the familiar quotation:

> "How now, brown cow
>  Grazing on the green green grass ..."

Now read the words not as signs but as sound-things:

> "h-OW n-OW brr-Ow nk-OW
> GRR-zing nth GRR  Een  GRR EenGR ASS..."

Now translate the sound-things into word-signs:

> "PAIN
> ANGER"

The last two statements, "Pain, Anger," is the meaning that an infant or a poet or perhaps also a schizophrenic might attach to the original line of poetry.

Some poetry, especially modern poetry but not exclusively (Blake, Donne, Shakespeare have also knowingly punned/word-played in this manner), challenging the reader to undergo this contextual transmutation as if he were precognitive or schizophrenic.

The unenlightened reader who does not undergo this process finds himself 'meaning-blind.'

The difference between a normal person reading "schizophrenically" and a schizophrenic reading "schizophrenically" seems to be simply this:  whereas the normal person can fluctuate in *set* from the original line to its contextual transmutation, and does this intellectually and voluntarily, the schizophrenic (presumably though not always) reacts in a nonintellectual, involuntary, reflex manner to the contextual transmutation *alone.* [Refer back to Broad, *supra,* for his discussion of the conditioned reflex as opposed to voluntary action.]

A further discussion of 'meaning-blindness' and its bearing on the phenomenological language of science, as well as the construction of more efficient scientific "mental models," will be the main topic in Part II of this paper.

PART II:  (Philosophy of Science)

(a) psychophysics and information science
(b) Caw's percept-term-concept scheme
(c) a discussion of the symbol
(d) meaning-blindness expanded
(e) language as a habit of reason

My use of the term 'mental model' as being the psychological counterpart of the neurological reception of phenomena is based on an enlargement of Caw's scheme of relationship between percept-term-concept to include what is psycho-biologically known about some of the processes of learning, perception, and cognition. (Peter Caws:, "The Philosophy of Science," VanNostrand. Princeton:1965)   The latter pertains to the field of psychophysics as combined with information theory.

Psychophysics is concerned with stimulus-response relationships; it also includes experiments in which the subject is called upon to identify stimuli, or to make absolute judgments. Information Theory explains how these judgments are arrived at through a reduction of freedom of possibilities of choice as determined by the relative frequency of a stimulus. This is especially obvious in certain formal aspects of verbal communication:

"Spoken language has various constraints inherent in it.  Generally the words we use at any given time determine to some extent, sometimes slight and sometimes considerable, the words that we shall use next…The context tells us something about the word to follow by reducing our freedom of choice as to the next word…This enables us to calculate the information that is provided by the context

25

about the next item. And when this item occurs, some of the information that it provides is the same information as that which has already been supplied by the preceding context...such redundant information is by no means...worthless." [W. Sluickin "Minds and Machines," Penguin. Baltimore:1960. (95)]

**This relates to Zipf's** (G.K. Zipf, "The Psycho-biology of Language," M.I.T. Cambridge:1965 (212-218)) **study of emotional equilibrium in language which is a statistical analysis of the rate of redundancy:**

"...in the vast majority of instances, everyday speech should represent the average rate of variegation, and should reflect the average rate of tolerable change...the meaning of arrange words must...strike the auditor as comprehensible, yet we select and arrange words not only to convey information but also to hold his attention. The curious orderliness which we have found in the distribution of words...reflects the orderliness of emotional change...Nothing would be more illuminating than a statistical investigation of the frequency-distribution of speech-elements in pathological language..." [G.K. Zipf, op cit. (212-218)]

**Information theory, which regards any organism as a transmitter and a receiver in a communication system, diagrams reception and transmission as follows:**

"Suppose now that we send a series of messages; let us call this series, *series x*.
If the channel along which the messages are transmitted were a perfect one, *series x* would arrive at the receiving end. But channels are often imperfect.
There may be some information lost in transmission; and some spurious information may be picked up. As a result, what is received is a more or less distorted series of messages; let us call this series, *series y*.
For any series of messages, the average information per signal is given by H;
The information per signal actually transmitted is given by T; its calculation is based on the frequencies of the occurrence of the signal. The quantities that may now be considered are as follows:

H(x), input information per signal
H(y), output information per signal
Hy(x), information per signal lost in transmission (equivocation)
Hx(y), information per signal added in transmission (noise)

The manner in which these quantities are interrelated may be represented in a diagram, as by G.A. Miller of Harvard. The total area of this diagram, denoted by H(xy), consists of the sum of information lost, transmitted and added." [Taken verbatim from Sluickin, op. cit., pp. 86-87. It should be noted that when dealing with information transmission in biological systems, the areas H(x) and H(y) represent multiple dimensions of both chemical and spatiotemporal interactions. The diagram shown above represents an expanded rendition from that in Miller.]

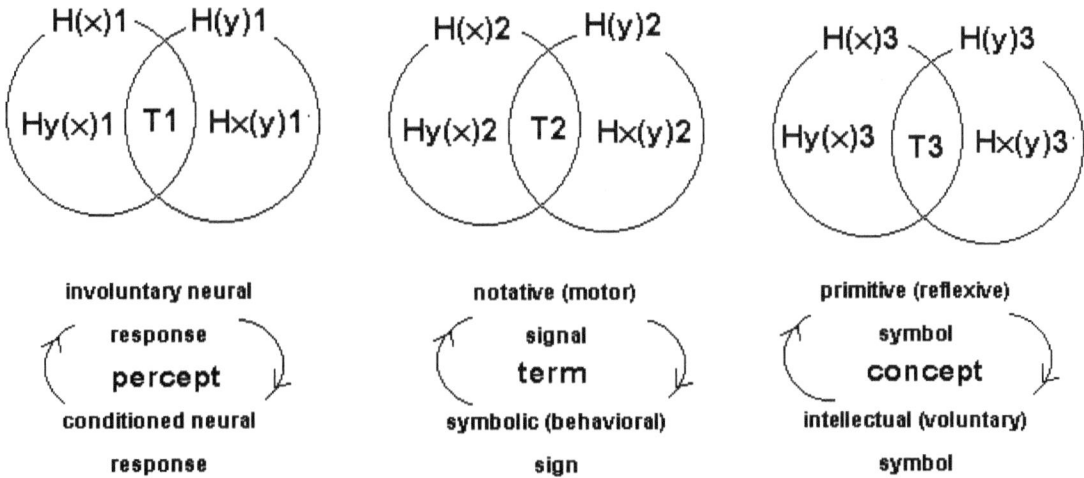

involuntary neural
response
percept
conditioned neural
response

notative (motor)
signal
term
symbolic (behavioral)
sign

primitive (reflexive)
symbol
concept
intellectual (voluntary)
symbol

The scientist's common sense assertion is that an isomorphic correspondence between percept, term, concept must be indeed roughly achievable in scientific discourse such that the informational content T can be preserved at T1, T2, T3, etc., thereby permitting reliable intersubjectivity of observation - otherwise, what point would there be in trying to communicate at all! [The percept-term-concept model referred to is taken from Caws, op. cit. Professor Caws is now much older and much wiser and although this earlier view is now entirely outdated post Wittgenstein, Quine, Feyerabend, etc., its elementary approach is still adequate for the discussion that follows.]

The parameters of observation, the material and mathematical instruments employed, guarantee a measure of hard-science consistency. Accepting this rough schematic, it is in the area known as noise - Hx(y) - on the concept side of the diagram - which I believe relates most to the formation of an 'irrational mental model'.

A discussion of how an 'irrational mental model' differs from the 'scientific concept' must take into account the conventional scientist's (i.e., early Caws') basic assumption that in the scientific mind the internal structures of the three segments (percept-term-concept) will exhibit at least a partial isomorphism, and that hopefully all three will also show some isomorphism with natural reality, although that can never be known directly.

Caws does however allow that the three segments can stand without the other two, although (in sane thought) this never lasts long:

"...in the condition known as *awareness*, in the course of many forms of *activity*, and in aesthetic experience, we are able to concentrate on perception to the exclusion of language and conceptual thought; the contents of perception are grasped in a form which makes them suitable for thought, without in fact leading to it, the experience being immediate and complete in itself.

"In logic, two systems are said to be isomorphic if every element of one system can be matched with a unique element of the other, and vice versa, according to some rule, and if furthermore every relation linking elements of one is matched by a relation linking the corresponding elements of the other" [Caws, op. cit. pp. 70-71]

It is *the rule of correspondence*, however, which I believe to be a key factor in determining the direction of an individual conceptual scheme. Note Wittgenstein's observation [L. Wittgenstein, The Blue and Brown Books," Harper & Row. New York: 1960 (37)] (echoed by Caws) with regard to the relationship between concepts and their corresponding terms, that models analogous to the original need not resemble the original in any way but are merely interpretations of the same calculus.

I believe it has been established that, ideally in scientific thought, the same calculus is used for isomorphically consistent translation of percept-term-concept. However, this need not be the case, especially in instances of selective perception. In my diagram I have therefore distinguished between the initial, involuntary reflexive neural response and the secondary, conditioned, selective neural response, which varies with each individual.

Likewise, the selective neural response corresponds to the primitive symbol. [See passage and footnote in Part I: from R. Marshall, unpublished notes for Master's thesis, Hunter College Psychology Dept., New York City; paraphrased from S. Ferenczi, "Sex in Psychoanalysis." (276)] which may be likened to a conditioned reflex from whence, through some complicated psychobiological process, the voluntary, intellectual symbol is derived. [The modern view, since then refined in my own paper on "self-consciousness" and the Split-brain research done by the Sperry team at Cal-Tech in the 1970's is that all intellectual activity is a motor activity in the brain, therefore entirely capable of quantification in 'the same calculus' as the underlying behavioral description.]

Similarly, the intellectual symbol assigns a corresponding term or terms in language which have linguistic meaning that then can be partially confirmed by perceptual reinforcement. However, if the calculus has not been rigidly consistent in any of these many transitions, perceptual reinforcement tending always toward the selective, the rate of human error increases.

My discussion of the 'irrational mental model' is primarily focused on the conceptual side of the scheme and depends heavily upon an investigation of the various levels of symbolism that seem to intercede between the states of perception and cognition. A large controversy exists in this area and I cannot hope to do more than enumerate some of the more prominent theories as to what constitutes the "symbol" in psychological terminology.

In nonpsychological terms, the symbol might be simply defined as the 'conceptual counterpart of the word-sign'. Dorothy Walsh differentiates between the two in an essay on the cognitive content of art:

> "A sign is a passageway to something else; it is a self-effacing means to some insight which lies beyond it. It is diaphanous and opaque. It does not point to something else; it holds its meaning within itself. The relation of the sign to what it signifies is a matter of convention, whereas the symbol must be, or at least must appear to be, the suitable and natural vehicle of the meaning which it embodies; that is, it must in some sense resemble what it means......Further, signs commonly belong within a system such that some signs may be substituted for others without loss of meaning, as 1 plus 2 is equivalent to 3, and a technical term is equivalent to its definitions. But symbols are commonly solitary and cannot be substituted for one another without radical change of meaning." [D. Walsh excerpted in Eliseo Vivas and Murray Krieger, "The Problems of Aesthetics," Holt, Rinehart & Winston,. New York:1960, pp. 612-613]

In a psychoanalytic sense, the meaning of the term 'symbol' depends largely on whether one is referring to the Freudian or Jungian usage.

Ferenczi, modifying Freud, calls it a "substitutive, illustrative replacement-expression for something hidden." [Ferenczi in Marshall, op. cit. p. 277] This is somewhat less sex-oriented than the sense in which more formal Freudians, such as Fenichel, define it:

> "For example, the idea of a penis may be represented by a snake, an ape, a hat, or an airplane, if the idea of a penis is objectionable. The symbol is conscious, the

symbolized idea is unconscious. The distinct idea of a penis has been grasped but rejected. [Fenichel, op. cit. p. 28]

**Perhaps the best clarification of the Freudian idea of the symbol can be obtained from Jung, who emphasized that Freud's method of investigation was confined to morbid psychic phenomena, whereas his own use referred primarily to 'archetypal' innate structures:**

"It is based upon the assumption that the neurotic patient is representing certain psychic contents from consciousness because of their incompatibility or inconsistency with conscious values...The unconscious background does not remain inactive, but betrays itself by certain characteristic effects upon the conscious contents...A most important source of the knowledge of unconscious contents is provided by dreams, which are direct products of the activity of the unconscious."

## However, Jung continues,

"Those conscious contents which give us a clue, as it were, to the unconscious backgrounds are by Freud incorrectly termed symbols. These are not true symbols, however, since, according to his teaching, they have merely the role of signs or symptoms of the background processes. The true symbol differs essentially from this, and should be understood as the expression of an intuitive perception which can, as yet, neither be apprehended better, nor expressed differently." [Jung excerpted in Vivas, supra. pp. 166-167]

**Apparently, Jung's use of the term 'symbol' is closer to Walsh's. To this might be added Fenichel's belief that symbolic thinking may be directed by the primary process, and is a part of the primal, prelogical thought process. [Fenichel, op cit. p. 28] And it is important also to remember Ferenczi's observations on the learning patterns of the infant mentioned in Part I. This last is especially important in that it seems to indicate that the preverbal concept carries with it an infantile, vestigial set of percepts which the adult refines or discards in consciousness but which may manifest themselves in dreams when the logical process relaxes.**

For example in the case cited earlier in Part I: "everything that opens is a door," the symbolic set might be represented as follows:

**key individual sense datum of the infantile learning set:** *DOOR*

**adult conceptual symbol**
**THE KINESTHETIC SENSE OF ALL THINGS**
**THAT OPEN AND CLOSE:** *box, book, closet, window, coffin, mouth, trunk, cabinet, etc...*

If the above scheme is valid, it may mean that in dreams, with the relaxation of consciousness, any one of the signs (book, box, etc.) which are vestigially connected to the adult conceptual symbol which, it may be noted, may be as much kinesthetic as intellectual, may appear in the dream as a substitutive replacement expression for "the sense of all things that open and close."

This hypothesis is inspired and built upon Ferenczi's landmark work in the language of schizophrenia and my own observations on the nature of metaphor and other poetic devices which seem also to derive their aesthetic significance from this prelogical tendency to identify and exchange objects on the basis of some infantile rule of similarity. [At the time of my first writing, c. 1963, work was already progressing in the psychobiological and behavioral sciences linking the production of speech to all other underlying kinesthetic/motor processes. Since then, the quality of speech (i.e., its precise logico-configurational fit within the continuous present of Self-Consciousness as a purely linguistic process) has been found to be precisely contiguous with all internal communication in the biological system and wholly dependent upon which areas of the body and brain are included in the kinesthetic information feedback loop. This early work therefore presages my post-1970 hypothesis that there is indeed a strict one-one correspondence between all brain states and mind states, connecting the entire realm of Mathematics as a graphic language to the field of "all that can be spoken."]

The following excerpt from Piaget's landmark empirical work on the language and thought of the child may add the missing link to this elementary discussion of the 'symbol':

"M. Janet...considers that the earliest words are derived from cries with which animals and even savages accompany their action...Hence the earliest words of all...are words of command. Thus the word originally bound up with the act of which it is an element, at a later stage, suffices alone to release the act. The psychoanalysts have given an analogous explanation of word magic. The word...having originally formed part of the act, is able to evoke all the concrete emotional contents of the act...(similarly)...the baby syllables, *mamma*,...are formed by labial sounds which indicate nothing more than a prolongation of the act of sucking. *Mamma* would therefore be a cry of desire, and then a command given to the only being capable of satisfying this desire. But...the mere cry of *mamma* has in it a soothing element; in so far as it is a continuation of the act of sucking, it produces a kind of hallucinatory satisfaction. Command and immediate satisfaction are in this case therefore almost indistinguishable…

"…the earliest substantives of child language are very far from denoting concepts…the fact remains that many expressions, which for us have a purely conceptual meaning, retain for many years in the child mind a significance that is not only affective but also well-nigh magical, or at least connected with peculiar modes of behavior which should be studied for themselves and quite apart from adult mentality." [J. Piaget, "The Language and Thought of the Child," Meridian. Cleveland:1966. pp. 27-28 By 1970, Piaget also did landmark work in Bioepistemology, connecting all biological processes to concept-formation processes, founding the developmentalist movement in psychology and bringing the notion of the possibility of finding a strict psycho-neural parallelism that much closer to general acceptance.]

Piaget's early study concludes that instead of the traditional view that the child's mental growth depends merely upon quantitative addition of experience, the development of language and thought is primarily qualitative - that the character of the child's mental activity alters in kind.

So much for a brief description of the 'symbol'.

I believe enough evidence has been presented here to argue that the correspondence between percept-and-concept, due to the qualitative variation of symbolic thought, need not be one-one but in fact more often takes the form of many-many.

While it is the scientist's hope that the relationship between percept-and-concept does follow the same correspondence rule as that which exists between term-and-concept, however I will endeavor to demonstrate how the influence of language can compensate for the lack of correct analogy between percept-and-concept, thereby enabling an irrational conceptual scheme belonging to either $Hx(y)$ or $Hy(x)$ to function rationally in certain overall areas of $H$ over a range $T_1, T_2, T_3$, etc. [The objective is not to demonstrate that scientific language can be irrational but rather that natural language, tending more readily toward the irrational, can still point to reasonable and more precise meaning in the languages of science.]

Therefore, returning to our previous diagram, let us investigate the informational relationship existing between concept-and-term.

Since context and discourse play a major part in the use of language to stimulate thought, it might be argued that on this side of the scheme the rule of correspondence lies *partially outside the mind.*

Likewise, it can be argued that the relationship between term-and-percept lies *wholly outside the mind,* as determined by social (i.e., intersubjective) norms, since a strictly 'private language' is nonsensical. [Since Aristotle (Post. Analytics II,9) and more recently after Russell, Wittgenstein and Quine, it has been demonstrated that all terms, including names, reflect a relation between universals of a lower conceptual order - the most primitive being the universal relations drawn between numbers as primitive 'names/signs' in Mathematics which, since Godel, has been shown to be an imperfect and hence equivocative open system.. This part of my argument is more extensively dealt with in subsequent papers.]

It is plausible to argue that the percept-concept relationship may be regarded as the hypothetical counterpart to the experimental activities of linking concept-term and term-percept. If the calculus, or rule, of correspondence that links concept-and-term is logically consistent with the one linking term-and-percept, the kind of intelligence which on the percept-concept side of the scheme is able to simultaneously hold a multiple of concurrent hypotheses, will be able through a process of private "asides" to eliminate all but the appropriate hypothesis consistent with the exterior calculus. Such a person would be partially "meaning-blind" in that he has negated the emotional content of the experience for the purely functional one of a conditioned response to a percept-term stimulus.

## Wittgenstein eloquently experiences this realm of "meaning-blindness":

"...the objection is that someone might...make the signs correctly in the 'game' with other people and get along all right, even if he were 'meaning-blind'...Could we not imagine someone who could make no sense of...a question? If you said a word to him...it gave him no meaning. And yet he could 'react with words' to the sentences and other utterances he encountered, and to situations too, and react correctly." [Wittgenstein, op. cit., Preface xv]

## Then, in a later section of *The Blue Book*, Wittgenstein hits the nail right on the head with respect to what "meaning" may signify in post-Piaget epistemological psychobiology:

"We could easily imagine beings who do their private thinking by means of 'asides' and who manage their lies by saying one thing aloud, following it up by an aside which says the opposite...(meaning, thinking, etc.) Why shouldn't they be the specific private experiences of writing—the muscular, visual, tactile sensations of writing and speaking?

"Let us sum up: if we scrutinize the usages which we make of such words (thinking, meaning, wishing, etc.)…going through this process rids us of the temptation to look for a peculiar act of thinking, independent of the act of expressing our thoughts, and stowed away in some peculiar medium. We are no longer prevented by the established forms of expression from recognizing that the experience of thinking *may* be just the experience of saying, or may consist of this experience plus others which accompany it." [Wittgenstein, op. cit. pp. 42-43 This passage is key to my own Information Science explication of the phenomenon of 'Self-Consciousness' later included in the many papers in this volume.]

**But this last excerpt is too ambiguous and falls into a language-trap that Wittgenstein probably also himself surmounted in later work.** *There must be more to the process of thinking than can be assimilated by natural language.* **Otherwise, the contention of the linguistic relativists that language can limit thought would extend to the language(s) of science, which it does not:**

"…(Basson and O'Connor) conferred with various linguists to determine if the perennial metaphysical positions and problems could be stated in different languages. They discovered that various metaphysics are, so far as language is concerned, equally at home in any culture. Finally, Hockett believes that 'scientific' discourse can be carried on in any language the speakers of which have become participants in the world of science, and other languages can become properly modified with little trouble'…" [Ernest Partridge, "A Preface to Linguistic Relativity," unpublished draft: 1961. P. 37 Undoubtedly Dr. Partridge, who was then a doctoral candidate kind enough to show me a draft of his dissertation, has gone on to publish many more brilliant treatises.]

**However, the contention that language can structure a *habit of thought* therefore leading to a *habit of reason* (or the use of a consistent calculus) I believe (especially since the work of W.V.O. Quine and the Behavioral Psychologists) is generally accepted.**

"The 'fashions of speaking' in a language are not patterns that *must* be used because no other modes of expression are possible; rather, they are patterns which are habitually used or used with greater ease than other patterns of expression." [Partridge, op. cit. p. 136]

**Partridge continues, holding language to supply the conditions of cognition, being one of the fundamental components and conditions of**

cognition itself. This I believe can be allowed, but only if one postulates the use of the same calculus for percept-term-concept. This is why the 'hard' sciences rely on the readings of 'instruments' (none-the-least of which being the slide rule and the measuring stick) whose construction and instruction for use are given by a theory that employs them as extensions (i.e., prostheses) of the Observer's 'eyes', 'ears', and 'language'.

But if more than one rule of correspondence is brought into play, such as when alternate observations generated by alternate instrumentation takes place, cognition alters qualitatively bringing about the experience of other, nonscientific, seemingly irrational universes that are perhaps closer to what may be termed Man's 'soul', to his capacity for 'feeling', but not to his struggle for survival through the meeting of Nature on its own terms.

It is in this larger range of self-communication that *metaphor* plays an important role in the concrete world of the Observer.

[This last sentence is recently added in order to transition to my subsequent papers where, post-Godel, metaphor is treated as a creative addition to an established linguistic convention.]

*ArtemisSmith* 1966

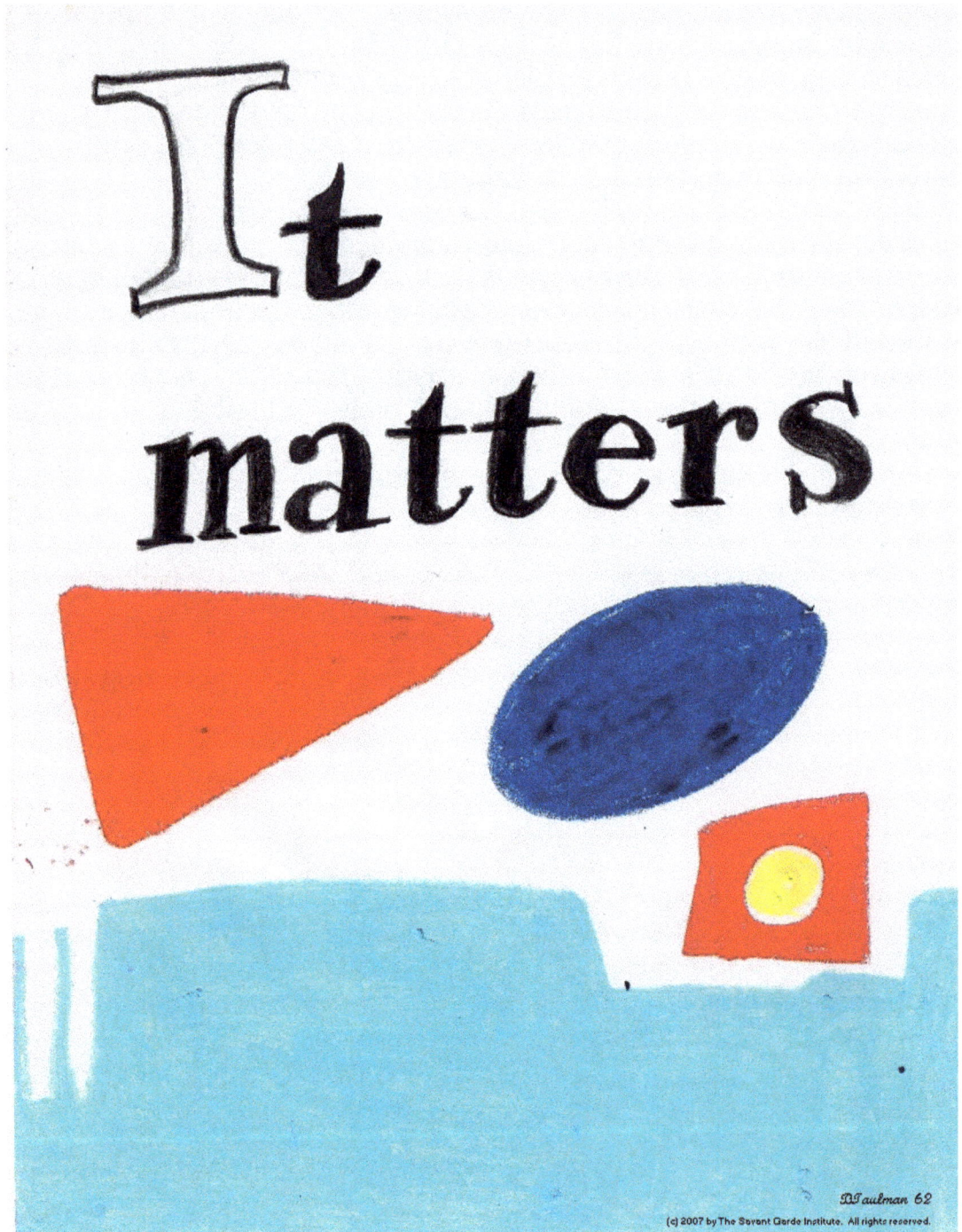

B. Taulman   crayon layout   1965

# 3. FUTURESEX: Human Sexual Evolution beyond the Species Level

This paper is now partially outdated, but has been reprinted primarily for its historical value and some of the insights it still may contribute. Please note that it long predates the media advent of "Dr. Ruth" as well as the published philosophical papers of Professor Thomas Nagel. It was globally distributed by members of New York Mattachine to academic reviewers, including Donald Webster Corey (a/k/a sociologist/criminologist Dr. Edward Sagarin at The City University of New York).

## ABSTRACT

An alternate proposal to the present concept of human sexuality stressing human sexual evolution beyond the species level, subsumable under the modern trend toward the unification of science. It is argued that the modern shift in the concept of mind toward theories of information exchange leads to a reinterpretation of all conscious experience as the result of communications-exchange processes, and that this is continuous with the reinterpretation of all physiological phenomena as information-exchange phenomena, under the unification of science. Accordingly, human sexual behavior, as a subspecies of psychobiological behavior, is reinterpreted as a communications activity. The sociological implications of this view are that sexual freedom may be held subsumable under present Constitutional guarantees covering higher forms of human communication. The evolutionary implications of this view are that human sexual activities, and the quality of the pleasure resulting therefrom, may extend well beyond the involvement of the natural sexual organs with which we are genetically endowed.

## Introduction.

The object of this investigation is to arrive at a reformulation of the concept of human sexual identity adequate to meet the requirements of today's trend toward the unification of science. The moral revolution has also awakened the need for a new philosophy of sex which takes into account the human rights of women and the sexual minorities. In the revolt against the old morality, there has been too heavy a reliance on the scientific and medical professions to dictate what the new morality should be.

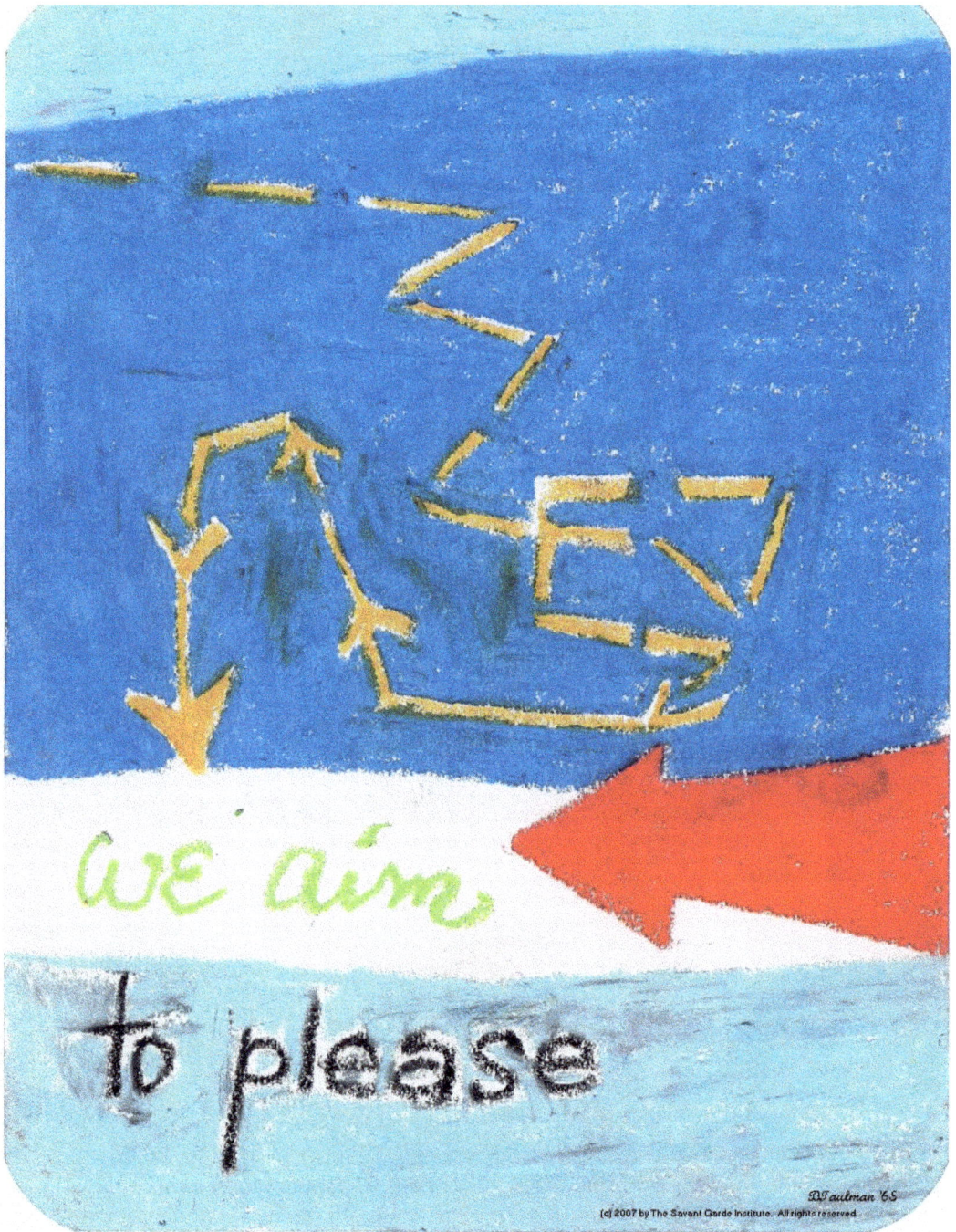

B. Taulman   crayon layout   1965

While a conscientious job of doing so often has been performed by physicians and psychologists, questions about what is truly moral are best answered not by science alone but by science and the value theorist.

In the past, mistakes have been made by scientists for lack of some central viewpoint - thus Freud, for example, evolved psychoanalytical approaches to both women and homosexuals which, though advanced and liberal for his time, were ruinous in psychotherapy.

This paper is one of a series written from a central viewpoint on the nature of conscious processes, based upon an information-science concept of mind, designed to aid both the scientist and the legal theorist by providing them with some philosophical considerations relevant to theory of value in their own, 21st Century idiom. It is also a proposal, from a multimedia artist working in philosophy, for a new concept of human sexual identity.


## I. The present concept of human sexuality.

The etymology of the word "sex" is from the Latin "sex(us)", akin to *secus, secare,* meaning to cut or divide. Its preferred lexical definitions are:

1. Either the male or female division of a species, *esp.,* as differentiated with reference to the reproductive functions. 2. The sum of the structural and functional differences by which the male and female are distinguished, or the phenomena or behavior dependent on these differences. 3. The instinct or attraction drawing one sex toward another or its manifestation in life or in conduct. 4. Coitus, *v.t.*

This common lexical definition is technically inaccurate from the standpoint of the life scientist who discerns in some lover, primarily bacterial, life forms more than two sexes (as much as ten!) involved in the reproduction cycle. It is also inadequate for the psychobiologist when considering behavior deviant from the normal behavior associated with structural and functional differences.

If the objective of the categories "male," "female," etc., is to divide the species into subspecies solely according to reproductive functions, then terms such as "homosexual," "bisexual," have no meaning when applied to humans; but these terms do not have meaning for the biologist (it is incorrect to refer to amoeba as "homosexual," to flatworms as "bisexual," since amoeba engage in "fission" and flatworms are "hermaphrodites"). Despite the fact that an analogy analogy of sexual deviance exists in lower animals, terms such as "homosexuality" are restricted to variance in human behavior involving sophisticated psychosociological functions above the reproductive functions (such as "love"), not clearly discernible in lower life forms.

Increasing psychobiological evidence that all mammalian sexual behavior is as much dependent upon chemical differences in the brain as it is upon the structural and functional differences in the reproductive organs has further rendered the primitive division along strictly external physiological lines highly arbitrary and, realistically, useless. The difficulty in drawing a clinical division raises the question whether any division according to "proper sex" in psychology and sociology is at all useful, and whether it would not be better to do away with sexual categories altogether in ordinary language.

Whereas in medicine the problem of who can and who cannot engage in a particular act of intercourse or reproduction is still an important though increasingly comples question (especially as sexual prosthesis in the form of surgery, test-tube incubation, or mechanical alternatives becomes perfected), the problem of isolating sex differences which are essentially relevant to sexual activity in humans would seem too technical a differentiation for everyday needs (I.e., to remind someone daily that they are male or female, "heterosexual." "homosexual," "bisexual," "asexual," "polysexual," etc., may soon be regarded as punctilious as reminding them daily that their blood type is Rh-negative or positive!).

A strong argument for retaining sexual distinctions in ordinary language is, however, that a consciousness of such distinctive characteristics is functionally related to the successful engagement in a sexual act. It is argued:

> If sexual activity, now admitted to be a normal and beneficial physiological function, is to be engaged in regularly and with mutual satisfaction, an awareness of the sexual characteristics of both partners must be psychologically maintained on a frequent enough basis to permit sexual attraction and stimulation to occur.

> It is further argued that thoroughly obliterating the difference between the sexes may lead to early sexual confusion resulting in a less-than-optimal sexual adjustment, thereby educating heterosexuals to become bisexuals or homosexuals.

But the question of what constitutes an optimal sexual adjustment is precisely the issue under investigation. It can seriously be counter-argued that the optimal sexual adjustment for one segment of the human population is detrimental to other segments, thus the educational problem is one not of teaching everyone to do one thing, but of enabling each to do "his own thing."

For the purpose of our investigation, however, we will assume that an awareness of the sexual characteristics of both partners is a necessary condition for the proper performance of a sexual act. What we wish to inquire is precisely which characteristics are to be isolated as distinctly "sexual."

## a. The problem of sexual objectification.

The problem of isolating objects, events, syndromes, qualities, from the environment is an epistemological one. It has two stages:

i.  the classification of "raw data" from the periphery of perceptual reception into alternate, hypothetical and cursory categories, each of which represents an equipossible interpretation of given data;  and

ii. experimentation with alternate hypotheses and selection of successful categories.

The activity of (i.) is perceptual, the finished products of (ii.) are concepts.  Objects are differentiated and recognized by this process, and regulate the formation of concepts.

Sexual differentiation in lower animals is a perceptual, not a conceptual, activity (i.e., dogs do not ask each other whether they are male or female, they "sniff each other out" and then react according to their chemical determinations). An analogy of sexually deviant behavior in lower animals does not occur because some dogs or pigeons have "homophile" feelings - that is, not because they happen to fall in love - but because of some gap in their perceptual activity, either innate or acquired through frequent proximity to members of the same sex.  Thus, two male dogs who would normally quarrel may acquire tolerance and even "friendship" for each other.  Such perceptual gaps may even occur interspecialy:  cats may become attached to mice, dogs may make sexual advances to people, etc.  It seems ridiculous to regard such perceptual confusion as sexually deviant behavior.  While there is certainly some conceptual behavior occurring in lower mammals, sexual neuroses involving moral conflicts are difficult (though not impossible, in the case of "shame" in dogs, and more notably in chimpanzees) to instill.

In the human case, our recognition of sexual difference seems to proceed almost totally through the application of concepts learned by rote and imparted without the use of perceptual examples. (Thus, we get our fingers slapped when, as infants, we attempt to explore ourselves or our siblings; anatomical differences are hidden from us by clothing and sexual differences are reintroduced as differences in attire, social roles, grammatical inflections.)

If sexual deviance is a learned rather than a natural form of behavior, improper concept-formation is its cause and notoriously improper concept-formation more frequently occurs when perceptual reinforcement, in the form of actual clinical experience with the objects talked about, is not provided. (Thus doctors, lawyers, carpenters do not become competent practitioners until some internship is undergone.) Only in the case of naturalists (i.e., some nudists) does sexual differentiation occur in the order of perception-conception, and there seems to be little problem among such naturalists about sexual confusion.

If the above are plausible assumptions, it would seem to follow that as the sociological picture becomes more "unisexual" due to the need to insure sexual equality for everyone in the society, the obliteration of artificial means for sexual differentiation must be accompanied by greater opportunity for direct perceptual differentiation to take place - if we want children to develop their natural sexual preferences.

This may not insure a completely heterosexual society, however.


## b. What is undesirable sexual objectification?

It can be argued that

> leaving children to their own perceptions without some conceptual guidance particularly of a moral kind is dangerously haphazard. Children left to their own devices are far more likely to grow into savages than into responsible citizens. A completely naturalistic rearing of children in naturalist families is due not to the degree of freedom such children are permitted, but rather that naturalists are highly-opinionated, rigid moralists to begin with! Thus, to avoid undesirable sexual development, perceptual exploration ought to be guided by correct concepts. The problem of determining which concepts are correct is one left to the value theorist, once the limits of pathological development are established by the clinician (i.e., it is up to the clinician to determine how much homosexual activity leads to a loss of potential for heterosexual activity, etc.).

**But**

it is difficult to see why there should be any restrictions placed upon sexual activity above and beyond the usual moral restrictions placed upon *any* pleasurable activity. We ought always to be aware of the consequences of our actions, and ought never to act in ways that degrade or dehumanize either ourselves or other human beings (and we might also add a concern for other species as well). Accordingly, learning the manners of sexual interrelation would seem to be an extension of learning the manners of all social conduct.

**This view is particularly appealing to the proponents of sexual equality. They argue that the adoption of optimum criteria for sexual objectification and sexual behavior, since it affects the life-style of every individual in a community, must take into account the civil liberties, rights, and universal human needs of each person in the community; thus, while some psychologist may argue that it is more sexually satisfying for the male to treat the female as a sexual object rather than as a sexual person, this kind of behavior is immoral and ought not to be condoned. (This has the effect of limiting satisfactory sexual intercourse exclusively to love relationships, where the partners spontaneously come to prefer treating each other as persons rather than as objects for sexual gratification.)**

**It would seem fair to argue that**

any criteria governing the social pursuit of human preferences would have to subserve considerations in both legal and moral theory. Thus, while most human beings would prefer to be economically well off, this does not automatically give them license to acquire either by conquest or by stealth their fair share of the world's goods.

Accordingly, it would seem proper to maintain that it is legitimate for legal and moral theory to prescribe what is *not* permissible in sexual behavior; what is immoral is whatever degrades or abuses one's own person or other persons; what is illegal is any act that infringes upon the civil rights and liberties of others, as prescribed by law. The imparting of sexual mores, as a part of the moral education of the child, must conform to these requirements.

**While we ultimately have no quarrel with this view, it presents some very fundamental problems, the first of which being the problem of how to reconcile moral reality with everyday existential exigencies. This is a problem that arises not only in sexual contexts but in all social contexts. More often than not,**

although we know what it is morally proper to do in a given situation, from an ideal standpoint, this is not what we choose to do - either because it is imprudent (and going against prudent choice is, in another sense, immoral) or because we follow much stronger emotional inclinations.

From the clinician's standpoint, healthy sexual behavior bears no resemblance to what is considered polite social behavior; persons who have this attitude in bed are very dull lovers. It is precisely because our western culture has adopted such a wholesome, moral attitude toward sexual conduct that sexual neuroses tend so frequently to arise in our society.

The moral view propounded above is not really different from that already endorsed by the three major religions, or by current legislation. The problems relating to sexual equality are not problems about how persons should morally relate to other persons, but rather problems about the definition of "female person," and "deviant person."

A double standard about what is "good" for men and "good for women is held to, and arguments presented against a unisexual standard are that the physical and emotional differences between the sexes would render such a standard oppressive to both. Against sexual deviants, the argument is that this deviant behavior is not "good" either for the deviant or for others to whom he might spread his affliction and ought, consequently, to be either cured or at least prevented from attaining overt expression.

The movement toward sexual equality concerns itself not with the elimination of puritanical attitudes toward sexual conduct but with acquiring both for women and sexual deviants equal protection under the law as is presently enjoyed by heterosexual males, by redefining the concept of sexually "good" practices.

It would seem therefore that the mere shift toward a unisexual standard in our society, while it would certainly improve relations between all the sexes, will not solve the basic problem of what really constitutes an optimal attitude toward sexual conduct, one that is not "against nature" in the more enlightened, modern clinical sense of the phrase.

[i.e., Lovers do not perspire together, they sweat; sexual conduct is not 'gentile' - although it may be gentle, it is just as often rugged, nasty, a release of aggression - it has the character of a sport rather than a parlor game, and what is permissible is what is sporting (and that does depend a great deal on the strength and skill of the players); even among persons who share a high degree of action, there is the tendency - the need, the lust, the temptation - to treat one's partner as object rather than as person.]

Sexual conflicts arise when we become aware of the contradiction that exists between what our moral sense tells us is a proper way to relate toward other persons, and our momentary desires which - when our partners consent to gratify them - makes them partners-in-crime. Thus we adopt the attitude: this is what we do in private, and the rest of the world need not know. The result is less than optimal, for it is accompanied by guilt, shame, remorse - and this is a result "against nature" if sexual behavior is a natural form of behavior.

## II. An alternate proposal.

What is sought for is some kind of criterion for proper sexual objectification which will not lead to the classification of obscene behavior, when engaged in by consenting adults, in private, and with no deleterious consequences therefrom, as immoral behavior.

Therefore it will not do for us to argue in the conventional manner that though obscene behavior is immoral, it sometimes fulfills a moral function (i.e., the release we obtain from "harmless" shameful acts, such as watching a boxing match or hiring a prostitute, leads to a reaffirmation of our moral nature when we confess our sins and determine to act morally in the future; likewise, better to hire a prostitute for our escapades than subject our loved one to such degradation). Such arguments are specious. In the first place, willfully committing immoral acts does not insure our greater morality in the future - rather, the contrary; we run the risk of establishing dangerous precedents, habits we will be unable to break. Secondly, the selection of one class of human beings, willfully and premeditatedly, rather than in the heat of the passionate moment, as objects rather than persons, is a far greater moral transgression than the original sin we are trying to avoid.

There can be no moral excuse in a truly moral society for the existence of prostitutes or boxing matches or any other institution that maintains social emotional equilibrium at the expense of some of its citizens. Such a state of affairs leads neither to sexual equality nor sexual freedom, only to the perpetuation of a slave class. One need not be a Marxist to perceive this clearly.

But the alternative to such a hardline moralistic view need not be a puritanical one. If some obscene behavior is not immoral, one may perfectly well be either a prostitute or a boxer, providing one freely consents to such behavior and is not economically driven to it, for then one is not being abused or degraded. (In some societies, such as the Babylonian, prostitution was part of of religious worship, the function fulfilled by priestesses who enjoyed a very high status in the community; under such working conditions, few persons would find cause to complain!)

What is to constitute "amoral obscene behavior" if the word "obscene" essentially presupposes an immoral situation?   We shall obviously have to redefine the word "obscene" at some point, but not until we have explored the category.   The existence of societies, both past and present, in which erotic behavior is regarded either as morally neutral or as an out-and-out good thing gives us some justification for maintaining that the concept of obscenity is a conventional one, even if most societies - if not all societies - hold some things to be obscene;  the question is not whether the category has a right to be in our vocabulary, but exactly what kind of behavior should be included in it and whether some of this behavior must necessarily include erotic behavior.

Let us allow that any act which degrades a human being is an obscene act; what is it about erotic behavior that is essentially degrading?

The answer, according to our present reasoning, is any behavior which results in treating a human being as object rather than as person.  But what if we are only *pretending* to treat someone else as an object - what if we are only playing?  The woman who dresses herself up as an ostrich, the man who permits his penis to be adorned with pecans and chocolate sauce, is not seriously saying: this is who I really am.  We err when we think that we unmask our real selves in bed; we do just the opposite - we engage in fantasy and masquerade.

It is important to distinguish between the acts that we perform in different contexts and *who* we are; we are not simply the sum total of our acts, though some acts - those willful, premeditated, truly immoral acts we perform not in play but in earnest with disastrous consequences either for ourselves or for others - are acts by which our own conscience and public opinion judge us to be human or something less-than-human.

Social and sexual free-play, sport, games, ritual, dance, theater, art, may all be seen as alternate forms of human recreation; they are expressions of our creative nature;  it is not only natural for us, but absolutely essential for us to diversify our lives, explore new avenues, think of new games to play. To do otherwise is to grow old and rigid, to lose our awareness of the present.

But the fact that we sometimes indulge in fantasy need not intrude upon the rest of our lives.  Why should a man who likes to pretend he is "masculine" and a woman who likes to pretend she is "feminine" act the part around-the-clock?  To do so is to engage in infantile behavior; there is a proper time to play, and a proper time to be serious.

We ought to unmask ourselves when we hop *out* of bed. As civilized beings, we are more truly our real selves when we are fully clothed in the vestments of our own choosing than when we parade in our birthday suits. Evolution beyond the species level begins with the assumption of such a viewpoint.

## III. Postscript on the unification of science.

Thus far the view propounded here has been confined to a nontechnical analysis of the present concept of human sexuality, in ordinary language. However, a much more fruitful approach to the creation of an adequate theory of human sexual behavior, for the future development of the species, may be given by its inclusion under the concepts of information theory. This alternate description may also have important consequences for present legal theory, for it may be possible, once a central view of the universe which gives an account of moral phenomena as well as physical phenomena within the scientific idiom has been formulated, to justify many of the current civil liberties claims of the sexual freedom movements under already-existing legislation.

In governments whose political structure incorporates a separation between church and state, and particularly in nations which hold to this separation due to the presence of powerful rival religions, each of which might transgress upon the rights of the others, it is fitting that the question of *what is moral* be relegated to a nonsectarian body of professionals qualified to determine axiological issues;  this does not mean a body of theologians delegated to the task of sitting at some form of religious congress, for such a body would no more be qualified to determine policy on moral issues by majority vote than the U.S. Senate would be qualified to determine, ultimately and without further recourse for appeal, the legality of its own legislation.

What would suffice to constitute fair representation for the views of each of the religions in such a nonsectarian body of professional axiologists is that, discrimination not being present in the hiring or appointing of such professionals, the personnel would be representative of the nation's conflicting ideologies.

However the formation of such a body, consisting of genuine professionals in axiology (rather than some legion of decency composed of prominent and pious community leaders who are mere amateurs at the task) depends upon the existence of a genuine science of morals, continuous and synoptic with the physical sciences.

Such a profession ideally would, just like the legal profession, lean for its determinations upon precedents and paradigms, but also upon the empirical determinations of the lower sciences and, where these conflict with older views, the task of such a body would be to formulate new compromises.

But the concept of what is moral, in a nonsectarian state, is a negative concept. Whatever is moral is that which is not expressly indicated as being immoral.

> (In our society, the concept of what is legal is analogously a negative concept: whatever is legal is that which the law does not explicitly forbid; this means (a) that a statement of the law, in formal language, exists on record, (b) that its application acquires a list of precedents which determine its future application in particular cases, (c) and that the law remains consistent with the entire body of law, as that whole body of law comes to be interpreted, in the future as well as in the present.)

From the standpoint of our present, highly inadequate moral legislation, the explicitness of the phrase "acts against nature" which precedes the enumeration of forbidden sexual practices, is questionable in that the sciences have long since rejected the concept of nature to which it pertains (moreover, it was not a nonsectarian concept to begin with). Accordingly, it may be argued that while it is perfectly proper for a science of morals to forbid "acts against nature," what constitutes the class of such acts must be determined by scientists.

It is doubtful, however, that a body of moral theorists drawing their conclusions in a manner continuous with the physical and sociological sciences would consider "acts against nature" of primary moral significance; scientists regularly act against nature, and boast about it; the entire concept of man's evolution beyond the species level is a defiance of nature.

Accordingly, a body of modern moral theorists would be much more likely to concern themselves with the determination of "acts against humanity."

This is not a departure from the real sense of the prior, religiously-oriented view, since it was formulated to serve the needs of an anthropocentric universe. The old sense of "acts against nature" includes the suppressed phrase, "of man." No scientist will argue with this reading; the question, however, of what is the real nature of the human species is an open one since, because of our highly adaptable nature, we are to a large degree in control of our own future.

a. The adaptational character of human nature.

Since the central characteristic of our scientific concept of human nature is its adaptational quality (intelligence being a subordinate concept in present theory, since intelligent behavior is an analogue of adaptational behavior), and the scientific concept of what is "good" for a species being point-for-point identical with what is "healthy" for the species, as empirically determined - the line of argument for justifying a judgment of what constitutes an "act against humanity" is whatever act either limits or impairs an individual's optimal physiological, psychological, or sociological function, thereby threatening his powers for adaptation (i.e., his freedom, as a being with self-governing powers of intelligence, to remain master of his own fate).

Questions about which are the particular "acts against humanity" to be forbidden become much less arbitrary and easier to handle from this viewpoint, since a large body of science exists to test and research our hypotheses in a reliable manner, even if conflicts between moral theories are still prevalent. As the unification of science becomes more and more complete, the future of negative concepts such as "what is moral" and "what is legal" is even more easily determined than that of positive concepts - since the main problem that science cannot solve is "what is true" in an absolute, intertheoretical sense, whereas the problem of "what is contingent," also a negative concept, is much easier (since whatever is not explicitly contradicted by the unified body of theory is, theoretically, still possible).

## b. Sexual behavior as a communications activity.

The descriptive level which holds the most promise for the unification of the languages of science is that provided by the information sciences. Therein, adaptational activity of all kinds, including the biological, is regarded as a *communications* process whereby information is assimilated from the environment by the adaptational unit, which then accommodates its further experimental acts upon the environment; through such probing, also known as perception, the adaptational unit is able to acquire those patterns of action which prolong its survival, by arranging its perceptual input into alternate strategies of action and selecting from among these, through a process of optimization, the appropriate response.

A truly detailed description of this view cannot be given here, but an interesting feature - for legal theory - may be found in the reinterpretation of sexual behavior as a form of *communications* behavior, and this may be used to illustrate the ways in which the unification of science may be able to resolve questions about morals in the near future; how soon this will happen depends entirely upon the liberal inclination of the courts.

It may be argued that all acts of sexual reproduction are acts of human communication, and therefore Constitutionally guaranteed. (They are also guaranteed by custom, but our objective goes further.)

The legal argument for legitimizing sexual deviance in any of its nondestructive forms follows from the above in this manner: all attempted acts of human communication which fail are nevertheless covered by the same Constitutional guarantees, just as an attempted act of free speech or free association, which failed, would still be covered. [The only attempted acts at reproduction not covered by the above would be those in which contraception occurred, since the intention to reproduce would be explicitly denied by the act of contraception.] The participants could argue that their attempted act failed because of an error in perception; they were unable to perceive that all the requisite conditions for reproduction were not present in the sense that the more important perceptual cues, those which enabled them to engage in a sexual act, were forcefully present so that the volitional aspects of the act were depressed, and were not present on other occasions when they were exposed to stimuli having other requisite conditions for reproduction but lacked the more important perceptual cues. A mistake in perception, unlike a mistake in judgment, is involuntary.

To illustrate the force of the above argument, we may take an analogous example. Suppose a physician were asked to testify in the defense of a man arrested for urinating against a wall in a back alley, after a policeman had followed him there and waited to catch him in the act. Suppose the physician were to offer the following explanation:

This man is a patient;

as a child he was improperly trained and as a consequence cannot urinate in lavatories - it is a psychobiological impossibility for him, due to his early trauma; he therefore urinates only in back alleys, after taking proper precautions at not being seen;

he must urinate sometime, even if he can hold himself for long periods, therefore he must sometimes break the law;

the policeman went out of his way to catch him;

his actions hurt no one and, in fact, were less offensive than the public defecation of pets on city sidewalks in full view of everyone;

the only way to correct his problem medically is to fit him with some ambulatory catheter which would almost immediately irritate him and lead to serious infections, thereby providing a remedy far worse than the original problem;

his recognition of lavatories and walls is perceptual, and he is perfectly aware of the difference between the two types of places, and what people are supposed to do in either place, but his personal associations with each place have been irreversibly transposed, so that his involuntary response is always inappropriate;

the fact that urinating is a controllable reflex act is immaterial, since it is nevertheless an act which must be performed at some time and can only be performed, by this particular man, outside a lavatory;

the fact that he always takes great care to find a lonely spot where no one will see him should indicate his willingness to obey the spirit of the law, even though he cannot obey it to the letter.

We would probably find the man 'not guilty', and the trend in current legal theory is to be more lenient in the case of sexual deviance as well. But the urination case seems more acceptable than the deviant's case in that we are already accustomed to the behaviorist's notion of stimulus-response arcs, and the problem of simple, straight-forward psychological inhibitions.

Sexual acts, because of their socially more complex structure, are problems in perception on a much higher level; not only the sexual deviant, but just about everyone, has a problem in their sexual perceptions (e.g., we all have our distinct "types" to which we are attracted, and those which we wouldn't go near under any circumstances). The fact that these are actually problems in perception rather than intellectual quirks is simply illustrated by the fact that there are many people (e.g. those our parents would like us to prefer) that we intellectually know we *ought* to be attracted to, but simply aren't.

Now that we have argued for the above view, however, we wish to point out that it is only an interim argument, less than an optimal one, that can be offered to secure civil liberties for the sexual freedom movements.

It is not optimal because it appeals to the force of involuntary acts, whereas the objective of any sexual freedom movement should be the finding of suitable arguments for holding that any sexual act performed in private, between one or more consenting adults, which does not have deleterious consequences either physically, psychologically, or socially for any of the parties, or their progeny, or the community, is perfectly moral and should be legal. Furthermore, Furthermore, for acts of this kind to be moral, they should be voluntary - the result of human optimal choice for all individuals concerned. Arguments of this

this kind, under the unification of science, would have to proceed from demonstrations that whatever act was being considered would not in any way impair the health of the parties involved, or the community, and would therefore not be judged immoral.

c. A humanistic analogue.

Any reference to the involuntary quality of a sexual act is most unsatisfactory for the *programme* of achieving human evolution beyond the species level.  If we wish to be masters of our own fate, we ought to also be captains of our own body; thus it would seem that relying upon the notion of mistaken perception, and erroneous attempts at reproduction, are degrading ways to justify the commitment of acts which are pleasurable, subjectively chosen, and in many cases are accompanied by the highest moral feeling of love for one's partner. To regard the sexual expression of love as an illness, due to perceptual malfunction, seems quite grotesque in view of the fact that the sexual expression of love is good for everybody, and its repression deleterious for most people in both a psychological and sociological sense. And even in those cases where the sexual expression of love has no concrete object (i.e., in those cases where one's partner is merely a stand-in fulfilling an organic need), it seems perverse and primitive to regard the satisfaction of a basic physiological function as, in itself, either moral or immoral - although its irresponsible release might be thus regarded (*i.e., such as in cases where both parties do not consent to it, or when one of the parties is fraudulently misled into thinking that a real expression of love is taking place*).

The objective of such a humanist *programme* for sexual freedom is not to provide a carte-blanche rationale for all forms of what is presently categorized as obscene behavior, whether deviant or merely lewd, but rather to draw an enlightened philosophical line between what are to be considered acts of sexual "fair play" and sexual "acts against humanity."  The latter are to be deemed obscene and legislated against, both with respect to their actual performance and to their promotion or advertisement in the communications media.  The result of such a humanist *programme* will be to limit, in the interest of public health, far more of what is already permissible under the present inadequacy of the law, than what it will permit.  Thus the objective of such a moral revolution will be the enlightened reorganization of social values with regard to sexual behavior, rather than the blind elimination of restrictions.

Looking now to the future, we may one day come to reject the argument propounded in (b) above as inadequate on the following grounds:

i. Though human sexual behavior is a form of communications behavior, its primary purpose is not reproduction, and if reproduction follows from such an act, it is either by accident (which can be corrected by way of abortion), or by erotic choice (i.e., reproduction through sexual intercourse is just another sexual game we play.)

ii. The class of sexually deviant acts which count as errors in perception are all those involuntary acts which violate the rules of sexual "fair play," and these are to be distinguished from a second class of sexually deviant acts which are volitional and performed as "acts against humanity," being errors in moral perception. The former are subject to medical treatment, the latter, subject to punishment.

It seems plausible to argue that human evolution beyond the species level will render reproduction through sexual intercourse an entirely optional act; accordingly, the whole notion of sexual division of the species along reproductive lines will be antiquated; there will therefore be no real reason for maintaining that reproduction is the purpose, overt or covert, of sexual behavior; and its subsumption under the notion of communication will render the concept of sexual intercourse as merely another medium for social intercourse.

The rules for "sexual fair play" will thus conform to the principles for what constitutes social propriety in general - mutual consent between social peers being the primary consideration (i.e., gaining the consent of a halfwit is not the same as gaining the consent of a social peer; thus it may be wholly immoral behavior for one or more sophisticates to entice a simple soul into an orgy, just as it is considered nonsporting for four card-sharps to entice an unsuspecting greenhorn into a serious poker game).

What will constitute involuntary acts resulting from errors in perception are those compulsive acts such as exhibitionism (unless the parties watching are consenting adults) now generally recognized as belonging to that class, except for deviant acts between consenting adults which, under the new formulation, would no longer be considered deviant acts; there would, however, be a public health clause covering some acts even when performed between consenting adults (e.g., the willful spreading of venereal disease as a sexual "kick" as has become prevalent among some highly promiscuous groups), and to guard against the exploitation of persons of low intelligence or the economically disadvantaged or the brain-damages (e.g., those persons who at present are exploited as prostitutes or in the pornographic trades).

However, the whole notion of what constitutes exhibitionism or sexual exploitation will be so liberalized as to present very little problem except in those areas where sexual conduct will be a definite threat to public health.

A greater emphasis in the new obscenity laws will be put against volitional acts resulting from errors in moral perception; this is because moral perception is not a reflex act but rather involves the higher-order integrative functions: it is a form of "seeing as," rather than a form of "seeing."

To see someone *as* a sexual object is different from reacting sexually to someone; we cannot control our reactions but we can, in the case of controlled reflexes, hold ourselves in until another consenting adult who evokes a similar reaction in us happens to come along; moral perception is the perception of objects as related to a particular "attention set" - that context of human interrelationships that marks us as social beings having a large degree of mutual respect.

The notion of punishment for failure to conduct oneself morally makes sense only if such punishment works to promote the retention of such an "attention set" as a primary context for social intercourse; since moral perception seems to be a natural phenomenon in most people, emerging during the course of natural psychological development, most of the emphasis on future moral education will focus not on the artificial imposition of such an "attention set" but on preventive educational measures to insure that the natural formation of such an "attention set" is not impaired by behavioral practices which would tend to depress it (e.g., to encourage children to mistreat animals would tend to generally dull their perception of others' pain, whether animal or human; to expose the unsophisticated to mass-media simulations of sexual orgies - especially those of a sadistic type - would be to teach forms of behavioral adjustment to analogous situations in real life, rather than merely to entertain).

In general, the guiding principle governing what is to be deemed morally neutral in situations involving social intercourse of a sexual type are those acts, and mass-media reenactments, which do not unduly stimulate sexual behavior in a community to the exclusion of other forms of social intercourse.

There are certain kinds of sexual practices which encourage promiscuity of a type not recommended for reasons of public health; there are mass media simulations which are decidedly pruritic and ought to be reserved for situations in which sexual intercourse is intended during or afterwards, rather than indiscriminately displayed.

Moreover, if the question of consent is of primary importance, as it should be, such practices and media programming should be made available only to the sexually mature. (This could be handled by giving out licenses, to persons who have undergone the requisite training in sexual behavior to understand and fully control the extent of their participation.)

d. Aesthetic, pruritic, or obscene?

It is hoped that by the adoption of a humanistic code of sexual behavior that the class of stimuli labeled pruritic or obscene will be so substantially revised as to present no problem for a professional association passing on moral issues.

The symbols of sexual play that we find today obscene will simply be relegated to the class of the comical in the arts, a form of buffoonery which no one takes seriously and carries no special onus of immorality for those who take part as performers.

The more serious forms of sexual interplay, such as is found in genuine art films, will remain relegated to the realm of the aesthetic in that they point not to the act itself but to what is communicated by it.

The real locus of obscenity in any given situation is not an act that is performed *with* another human being, but rather that an act is being performed *against* another human being or group of persons.

We are justified in reacting with horror at a display of pornography today simply because we are aware that the participants are being degraded and dehumanized; this is not due to the acts they are performing, but society's attitudes toward those acts and the persons who perform them. We are all well aware that there can be no moral excuse for treating any portion of humanity as sexual objects in earnest rather than in play - and encouraging these to be used, abused, and shut out of the moral community for "permitting" themselves to be thus exploited, when such "permission" is not free consent but a socially-imposed pattern of sexual behavior and sexual identity which the ignorant victims of social degradation mistake for a real reflection of their "inferior" moral nature.

And even as we point to the prostitute, the deviant, the nonconforming female, as engaging in moral impropriety, we condone wars, prejudice, ghettos, and hard-core poverty, without going into equal reactions of visceral revulsion.

The conditions of present morals legislation work to create conditions which are not only obscene but genuinely atrocious. Any approach to finding ways of justifying human sexual free-play which does not result in the dehumanization of a large portion of the players should be most welcome; its overall effect on the morals of the community should be cathartic.

The advantage of the communications-theory approach to this problem is that it enables us to give an account of sexual intercourse which transcends the primitive biological stratus of purely physiological activity and brings sexual behavior, in humans, in line with the rest of human symbolic behavior.

All human sensorimotor activity is perceptual and leads to intellectually integrated concept-formation. There is no fundamental difference in the intellectual content of information gained through the use of one set of senses rather than another.

Sexual concept formation, and the perceptual activity which gives rise to it, is primarily one of tactile orientation. (The fact that we come to learn the differences between objects first through the use of our tactile sense, even as we learn to distinguish them with our eyes, tends to give us the subjective impression that this sense has a more basic ontological significance for us - objects learned by touch are more "real," more "concrete" than those learned primarily by sight or hearing, and are consequently "less symbolical" on a subjective level.)

Tactile perception, which requires greater proximity to the object, and has a completely different temporal spread than our faster senses (i.e., it is much faster to see or hear a phenomenon, as a *Gestalt* of a certain kind, than it is to touch it), is nevertheless a form of perception requiring as much intellectual integration as any other kind, and is subject to intellectual sublimation just like all our other senses.

We come to "see" a touched object *as* an object of a certain kind or another kind. The *communications* aspect of sexual behavior is precisely our coming to "see" ourselves and our partners primarily by touch. The fact that sexual satiety depends not only on the performance of such sensorimotor accommodatory activity, but on the degree to which we are able to integrate it intellectually into some kind of image or fantasy, corroborates this view.

The question of human evolution *to* the species level, in the sexual case, may have been one of coming to "see" the objects of a sexual act as objects of a sexual kind, belonging to living bodies capable of an awareness of their potential for sexual pleasure.

The question of human sexual evolution *beyond* the species level may turn on whether the objects of a sexual act come to be "seen as" objects of higher-level communication, belonging not only to a living body but also to a social and moral being - with whom we are actively engaged in an act of preverbal communication, a denotation activity in which the objects pointed to are not the objects "seen" by touch but objects of a much more complex kind.

The fundamental type under this kind of symbolization activity falls is no longer the merely "sensual," but the "aesthetic," and, in the case where the moral relation that subsists is highly prevalent in awareness, the "beautiful."

*ArtemisSmith* 1965

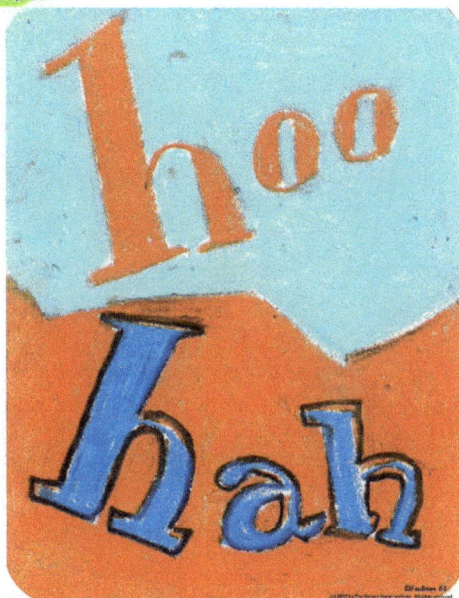

B Taulman crayon diptych 1965

Catch Me

I am a

Fleeing Thing

within my

Throbbing Core

a zillion lives exchange

from Cell to Cell

a Fluid

a Solid

a drop of dew contains

from Seed to Seed

Growing Spore

within my

Swelling Thing

I am a

Hold Me

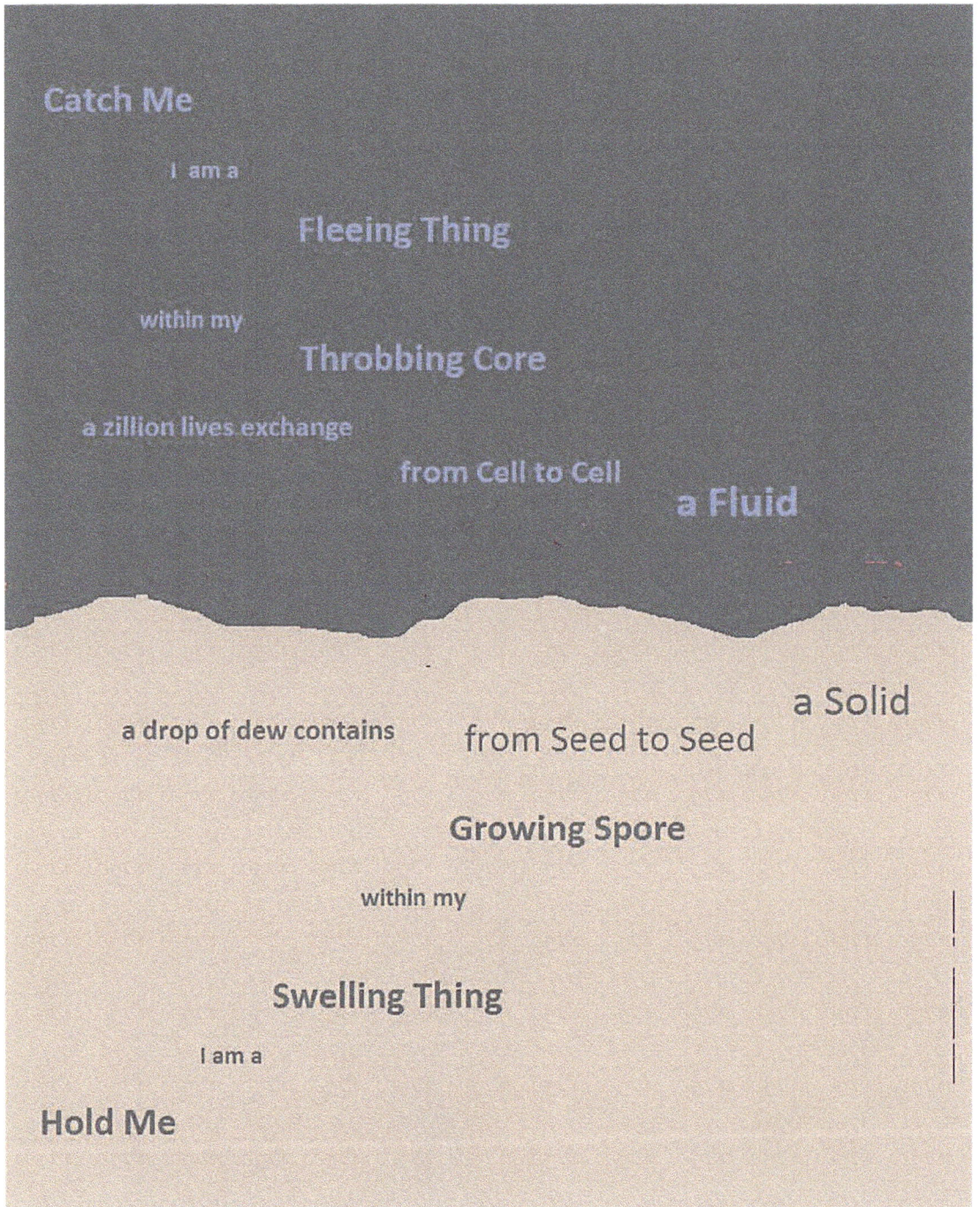

ArtemisSmith    Detail from "PteroDARKtyl Opera"    1965

# THE NEW GEOGRAPHY OF CONSCIOUSNESS

"This article was first commissioned by *Esquire* Magazine in 1969 which paid me to fly to Pasadena to interview the Split-Brain Research Team at California Institute of Technology. After much back and forth delay on the part of Cal-Tech, the faculty-approved article was submitted to *Esquire* and rejected by the Editors. *Esquire* left me free to market the article elsewhere and I immediately sold it to *The New York Times* which also paid me for it, then the *Times* Editors strangely decided not to publish it after all. A few months later the *Times* reassigned the article to another feature writer and published that version instead - which was simply a rewrite of an earlier article penned by Dr. M.S. Gazzaniga in another major publication. After years of delay, in 1981 Sperry, as head of the Cal-Tech Split-Brain Research Team which included neurosurgeon Joseph E. Bogen, was finally awarded the Nobel Prize for his work on divided consciousness. Reproduced below is tell-tale correspondence from Dr. Bogen, who later adopted the title "The New Geography of Consciousness" for one of his own scientific publications.

"In the period 1970 through 1978, I presented many of the papers reprinted in this volume at major philosophical and information science conferences as a featured speaker and was very well received. Having sent papers to some, I was also globally in touch with Nobel Laureates whose positive correspondence hinted at my being a Nominee for some distinguished prize and some Faculty at C.U.N.Y. were urging me to transfer to another more receptive university doctoral program such as Cal-Tech. Family responsibilities did not permit my applying to Cal-Tech but I applied to both Princeton and M.I.T. and was rejected. Concurrently, as a *stringer* for *SCIENCE & MECHANICS* Magazine, I was paid for numerous articles that the Editors failed to publish. I was also not reappointed as an Adjunct Lecturer at C.U.N.Y.'s Queensborough Community College despite having a substantial student following, and simultaneously dropped from the Doctoral Program in Philosophy at the C.U.N.Y. Graduate Center allegedly for having failed an examination that the Doctoral Faculty had voided. Despite all this, Civil Rights actions in both State and Federal Courts against C.U.N.Y., its Union, Princeton, M.I.T., and the E.E.O.C. all proved futile. Further, after my repeated demands for an investigation, Professor Mary Mothersill, head of the American Philosophical Association's *Committee on the Status of Women* reluctantly assigned Professor Jane English to investigate the reasons for my difficulties with academic re-employment within C.U.N.Y. and concluded in an open letter to Mothersill that all those reasons appeared to be "political."

"It should also be noted that in the period 1966-1973 the CIA and NSA had notoriously infiltrated both the Philosophy and Psychology professions and were actively interested in top-secret experiments in "*the explanation, prediction and control of conscious processes*," which formed the nexus of my dissertation proposal on the simulation of 'Self-Consciousness'. During that time, I was repeatedly invited to enlist in the CIA by C.U.N.Y's Personnel Director, Dr. Roberta Baker Thornton, who later indicated her eagerness to testify in Federal court if under subpoena. For personal reasons which she fully knew to be of the *Don't Ask, Don't Tell* kind, I had repeatedly declined. But the matter was never permitted to come to trial, and in one instance the presiding Justice "broke his leg" on his way to the State Courthouse and was replaced by one who delivered a 'bench dismissal', and another Judge, in Federal court, who was rumored to have been seduced in Chambers by a prostitute gaining access by posing as an attorney – also 'bench dismissed' my case on the eve of trial for lack of evidence which the C.U.N.Y. Faculty suddenly "could not locate."

"Strange psychological games were also being played on me by complete strangers who approached me with 'insider' information, as others had approached Taulman years earlier. Many of my academic sponsors, including Jane English, also subsequently suffered suspicious and untimely deaths and/or disappearances…all of which seems appropriate to mention in this Manifesto. It may be impossible to fully determine Truth from Conjecture at this late date in History, but much substantiation sits and waits in my collected papers for others to inspect and cross-reference."

*ArtemisSmith* 2015

ROSS-LOOS
MEDICAL GROUP
40th Year

# Ross-Loos Medical Group
947 West 8th Street
Los Angeles, California 90017

August 8, 1969

Miss Artemis Smith
8B-S
305 East 72nd Street
New York, New York  10021

Dear Miss Smith:

It was a pleasure to read the initial draft of your article, "The New Geography of Consciousness". (This seems to me an admirable title--can I ask, where did you get it?) I particularly enjoyed your discussion of what makes a whole man, in connection with W.J.--this was on page 12 as I recall. It is really great stuff.

It may take quite a few drafts back and forth to keep everybody happy, but you should eventually have a really worthwhile essay.

Best regards,

Joseph E. Bogen, M. D.

JEB/emt

# 4. The Split-Brain Phenomenon (THE FIRST DRAFT)
## (The New Geography of Consciousness)

"I believe to prove that each cerebrum is a distinct and perfect whole, as an organ of thought, and a separate or distinct process of thinking may be carried on in each cerebrum simultaneously..."

"Duality of Mind," A.L. Wiggan, Physician, 1845.

In the foothills below Mount Wilson Observatory, unobtrusively set among the rambling estates of quiet Pasadena, are the many laboratories of California Institute of Technology. Cal-Tech is most famous for its research in the physical sciences, yet the Institute is also a focal point in studies pertaining to the behavioral fields. Here a team of psychobiologists have established what "eccentric" Dr. Wiggan envisioned over a hundred years ago – the split-brain phenomenon.

A psychobiologist studies the mind by way of the brain. His experiments with lower animals usually involve surgical techniques, and one of these is the split-brain operation. The brain can be split because it is a double organ, its two sides intimately joined like the two segments of the heart. When surgically divided, each half of the brain continues to work on its own. Some years ago it was discovered at Cal-Tech that this kind of surgical division, when performed in humans, resulted in the emergence of two distinct centers of conscious intelligence.

I first learned of the split-brain phenomenon during an interview with Professor Beatrice Konheim, physiologist and academic dean at Hunter College's Institute of Health Sciences. She was the first to give me a composite picture that might explain why dividing the human brain results in the emergence of two individual minds, each with its own thoughts, learning strategies, and perceptions. Fascinated, I went to Cal-Tech to interview scientists, surgeons, and patients.

It all began in 1961 when it seemed that a new treatment for serious epilepsy had been discovered. A team of neurosurgeons from the California College of Medicine consulted with a psychobiologist, Dr. R.W. Sperry, head of the behavioral science team at Cal-Tech.

In one of his research papers, Dr. Sperry had noted that some of the monkeys being used in learning-theory experiments which had previously suffered from epileptoid-like seizures, were much improved after split-brain surgery. Naturally this had caught the eye of the medical profession which is always on the lookout for new techniques for treatment.  In animals, the after-effects of split-brain operations are almost negligible and they appear normal, making this seem a most desirable alternative for more drastic surgical procedures performed on severe cases of human epilepsy.

Known medically as *cerebral commissurotomy*, the procedure entails cutting down through the brain midline, severing the right-left cross-connections between the two cerebral hemispheres which, in epilepsy, often amplify and spread the attacks to both sides of the body.  This results in a doubling of the organ of consciousness, in the same way that separating the two sides of the heart results in two independently-functioning organs of circulation.  In both cases, some connections are left intact, yet in the case of the brain the division is sufficient to bring about a doubling of the patient's awareness – a fact which emerged as an unpredicted side-effect of the first surgical operation done in 1962.  Yet commissurotomy was otherwise highly successful in arresting the advance of grave epileptic seizures, so that to date, about fifteen human patients have chosen the acquisition of twin minds in preference to death or total debilitation.

What does one mean by "doubled awareness"?  Specifically, that the original consciousness of the patient has been divided in half, so that now each side of his body experiences a separate set of thoughts, learning-strategies, and conscious existence.  Because this contradicts all our common-sense convictions about the uniqueness and inviolability of the mind, as somehow a part of the "soul," this fact may take a long time to sink in.  To understand why such a thing can happen, it is necessary to know a great deal about the brain, and the scientific connections now being drawn between mind and body.  The major breakthrough in modern behaviorism is the realization that consciousness cannot be ignored in neurophysiological descriptions, and that the *quality* of awareness is an important index to the nature of brain function.  Moreover, the mechanism determines the kind of *mind* that emerges.

When a specific part of the brain is damaged or surgically excised because of tumors, a person becomes unable to engage in specific types of thinking or motor behavior which he as previously able to perform.  One can say, naively, that he loses some of his former aptitudes, and sometimes, also some of his former awareness.  Such aptitudes are correlated with the proper function of specific areas of the brain, not exactly in one-to-one fashion but nevertheless adequate for making medical diagnoses.  For example:  in the right-handed individual, the main language and mathematical aptitude centers are located in the left cerebral cortex. Lesions, growths, or chemical imbalances in these areas result in various kinds of speech defects; surgical removal of the cortex containing these centers (done in the event of malignancies) renders the patient unable to utter complex sentences.  While he may retain his ability to recognize objects and their names, he is no longer able to form sentences containing verbs. Moreover, even if the patient was an accomplished mathematician before the operation, this may result in his inability to solve even the most simple arithmetical problem.

In the temporal lobes of both halves of the brain can be found the various association centers that help us recognize and qualitatively discriminate what we see, hear, and read. Lesions in these areas can prevent a man from recognizing familiar objects or persons, or from understanding the written or spoken word.

Even psychological changes may be induced. Electrical stimulation of the cortex during brain surgery, while the patient remains conscious, has revealed special centers wherein memories and attitudes may originate. Vivid flashbacks of perceptual experiences can be evoked by the brain surgeon. The patient recalls past scenes in great detail together with all the thoughts and feelings he had experienced on that occasion, which he has since long forgotten. In other areas, electrode stimulation can cause the patient to assign a different *interpretation* to a present-tense situation; this means that an attitude change to his surroundings has been elicited, so that he describes his perceptual field as "strange" or "familiar," depending upon where his cortex is stimulated.

Physiological descriptions are not adequate to account for such effects. Communications theory models of information feedback between all the centers of the brain, as well as its connection to the rest of the body, must be employed. For this, the cooperation of the computer scientist is needed. Cybernetic models have been developed which tend to regard the brain as a vast, self-programming network of interrelated organic activity, far more intricate than the entire switching complex of the Bell Telephone System. (The entire brain operates on only about 10 Watts of electricity!)

This information network is only a *partially* printed circuit, which progressively becomes more determined as physiological *learning* takes place. This learning depends on the anatomical layout of the cells and on genetic and chemical processes of a more diffuse kind, all of which are influenced by the history of previous information input, which is thought to progressively determine physicochemical structures that at first are flexible and equipotential; this progressive determination is what constitutes psychobiological *learning* and *development.*

For example, an information impulse from the sense organs, which may or may not finally result in a conscious experience, is propagated in a highly specific spatiotemporal pattern of electrical and chemical discharge, to exact receiving points throughout the body. Triggered by such signals to produce more signals of their own, these receiving points respond by producing more nerve impulses or chemical substances such as hormones, which in turn act as signals to other target organs throughout the body. Each circuit reverberation influences the path of further circuit reverberations, altering the overall program of the mechanism. Feedback and information storage through this system seems to make possible all the most complex and coordinated of human actions, including abstract thought.

When the normal path of a signal through the cortical region of the brain becomes temporarily distorted due to interferences in the field (such as produced by scar tissue) an epileptic seizure may result. These are characterized by a fleeting hallucinatory experience, then unconsciousness and convulsions which can range from mild to very severe. Treatment for advanced epilepsy usually involves excision of those cortical areas which are causing the attacks to take place. Yet when vast areas of the cortex are involved, such surgery would not benefit the patient. In this instance, the split-brain technique may be used.

Cutting the neuronal "wires" that connect both parts of the brain to each other interrupts the path of signals of abnormal origin, so that they remain confined only to one side. There they eventually die down, and the patient becomes more responsive to medication that prevents the milder seizures from taking place. However, cutting these cross-connections also results in isolating one set of intellectual functions from its complement in the other side of the brain. With the organ of consciousness thus divided, information integration and feedback remains contained within one hemisphere, creating two centers of awareness in the patient, only one of which can express itself verbally because it, and only it, has the main aptitude centers for speech.

Back in 1961, when the split-brain research was confined to lower animals, no significant speculations were being made on whether monkeys used in experiments had acquired two centers of consciousness. Sperry and Dr. Ronald E. Myers, another psychobiologist then connected with the research team, were studying the mechanism of learning and sensorimotor perception. Their work was supported by grants from the National Institute of Mental Health and the H.P. Nixon Fund at Cal-Tech. They found that the animals' abilities to learn tasks was greatly enhanced by the operation – in that each side of the monkey brain became able to assimilate different and even contradictory information at the same time.

At that time, one of the neurosurgeons at the California College of Medicine had a patient suffering from violent and advancing seizurres, whose only hope seemed to lie in a cerebral commissurotomy. This was a World War II veteran who had developed the disease after a bad parachute fall and then also suffering repeated blows to the head while a prisoner of war. He strongly requested to be the first human subject to undergo the operation.

Even so, the doctors deliberated for almost a year; then, when it seemed that the patient's condition was truly critical and that he might well die from the force of the seizures which occurred as often as fifteen times a day, with a minimum of three major spells a week, the doctors finally decided to go ahead. The operation took place at White Memorial Hospital in Los Angeles.

After surgery, the patient seemed relatively unaffected, as the scientists had predicted from their experience with the split-brain monkeys. He even jokingly complained of a "splitting headache." His behavior was normal and he soon returned home to his wife, his epilepsy greatly reduced. During the next seven years he did not have a single major convulsion.

However, the research team at Cal-Tech which then also included Dr. M.S. Gazzaniga, requested the patient's cooperation in follow-up psychological tests to determine in more detail what the functional, behavioral, and neurological effects of splitting the human brain might be. It was during these tests that the doubling of his consciousness was discovered. Only then did certain puzzling behavior that the patient was experiencing at home finally receive a proper explanation. In the words of Dr. Sperry,

> "During the first half year after surgery, particularly with the first patient, we got reports suggesting that the disconnected hemispheres might each have a will of its own, and that the two occasionally got into conflict with each other. For example, while the patient was dressing and trying to pull on his trousers, the left hand might start to work against the right hand, to pull the trousers down on that side. Or, the left hand, after just helping to tie the belt of the patient's robe, might go ahead on its own to untie the completed knot.
>
> "The patient and his wife also used to refer to the 'sinister left hand' that sometimes tried to push the wife away aggressively at the same time that the hemisphere of the right hand was trying to get her to come and help him with something."

Since the first operation in 1962, most of the other epileptics who have undergone split-brain surgery have cooperated extensively with the Cal-Tech research team who have put them through a barrage of psychological experiments in which a controlled "conflict of the wills" is set up for the purpose of studying the nature of the mind in the silent hemisphere. Experiments follow a general pattern: some technique for interrupting the normal avenue of external external communication between the two minds (which normally keep in touch with each other by numerous outside "cues") is adopted, then the two sides are given contradictory information; the patient's behavior is subsequently studied to determine the extent and quality of intelligence in the silent cortex, as well as its language-comprehension abilities.

For example, in one of the earliest series of tests conducted on a housewife in her mid-thirties, who has been able since surgery to run her house, do the family cooking, go to market, watch television, all without complaining of any "splitting" or "double exposure" in her perceptual experience, the team of psychobiologists found plenty of evidence that her mute hemisphere really does perceive and comprehend on its own, even though it cannot express verbally what it sees and thinks.

Her "minor half" was able to read words like *cup, form,* or *apple* when these were flashed exclusively to its visual field; it indicated its comprehension by picking out the corresponding correct object with the left hand. While the left hand and its hemisphere were thus performing accurately, the opposite side had no idea which object or which picture or which name was the correct one, and made its ignorance clear through verbal and other responses. In such tests, the researchers had to convince the talking hemisphere to keep quiet and let the other side go ahead on its own, in which case it usually picked out the right answer.

In another early experiment the contrast between the information assimilated by the two sides was even more dramatic. The word *heart* was flashed across the patient's visual field but in such a manner that only half the word was projected to each visual cortex. When asked to tell what the word was, patients reported they had seen "art." But when they were asked to point with the left hand to one of two cards – "art" or "he," to identify the word they had seen, each patient invariably pointed to "he." This was a clear indication that the minor hemisphere, having access to only partial information, was working independently.

How independent was the other side of the brain? The next group of tests focused on whether it could also initiate its own emotional responses.

To determine this a pin-up shot of a nude was interjected in a series of neutral, nonemotional stimuli reaching the mute cortex. Under these conditions the talking hemisphere reported that it only saw a white light. Yet, as the next flashes continued, a slow grin would begin to spread over the subject's whole face, then blushes and giggles. The tone of the voice speaking for the major hemisphere was also affected although when asked what it was grinning about, it would reply that it had no idea, or would exclaim: "That's some machine you have there!" or "Wowee – that light!"

Apparently, only the emotional tone got across to the speaking half of the brain, without its cognitive aspect. This was also evident in other tests where the the minor hemisphere frequently triggered emotional reactions of displeasure by frowning, wincing, negative head shaking, and the like, whenever it heard the major side make stupid mistakes – in other words, when the correct answer was known only by that half of the brain.

During my visit to Cal-Tech, I interviewed two of Dr. Sperry's junior associates, Drs. Jerre Levy and Colwyn Trevarthen. Dr. Levy had just done her dissertation on the split-brain patients. Her experiments revealed the mute half of the brain to be a distinct entity that resembles the mind of a person who lacks the cortex with the main language and mathematical centers, due to surgical removal because of tumors.

"There is an intelligent and integrated, conscious mind there that can solve problems and feel its own existence, but just can't express itself verbally like the other side can," she stated. Moreover, although the other side is dominant for language, the mute hemisphere seems dominant for *Gestalt* perception – the ability to extract the configurational properties of objects. This special ability is the type of talent required by artists, sculptors, architects, engineers, and others who have excellent visual aptitudes. Thus she speculates that people in general might be classified into two categories: either 'minor hemisphere' types who are excellent visualizers, or 'major hemisphere' types who are great verbalizers and analyzers. If this is in fact the case, it will have great bearing on modern theories of education.

Dr, Trevarthen's research centers on visual perception. His complex findings reveal this to be a creative process of rendering visual information in a variety of alternate was, only a few of which reach consciousness. The primary perceptual structurings remain below the threshold of awareness.

I asked Dr. Trevarthen whether the difference in aptitudes in the two sides of the brain might not lead to two distinctly different qualities of awareness in the separated cortexes, which might reflect complementary aspects of the patient's personality.

"Any appreciable difference in the active strategies of perceiving within the mind will certainly lead to a different quality of consciousness," he replied. "The two halves of the divided brain may well see the world and its tasks and problems uniquely."

Yet he added that his work had also concentrated on determining what unifying factors between the two cortexes might be present in those lower regions of the brain stem which the surgeons had left intact. It seems that in those regions there is an underlying, unsplit subconscious vision which regulates the detailed conscious visual perception in each hemisphere. The two visual consciousnesses, although they may be qualitatively different, are not entirely free of each other. They seem to be coordinated by undivided parts of the brain.


My next interview was with Dr. Joseph E. Bogen, one of the members of the surosurgery team headed by Dr. Philip Vogel. We met in his office at the Ross-Loos Medical Group in Los Angeles. Dr. Bogen is a plain-spoken, shirt-sleeve physician who runs his practice like an old-style family doctor. His patient, the war veteran, was the first man to be operated on. Since then, Dr. Bogen has assisted Dr. Vogel in about fifteen other cerebral commissurotomies.

I asked him what kind of patient would be considered eligible for this kind of surgery. He went through the list of those accepted thus far; in most cases, the history reads the same:

brain damage at birth or early childhood with subsequent appearance of severe epileptic seizures that continue to worsen despite all medication. At least three of the patients were in their teens at time of surgery; the others were in their thirties and forties. The after-effects seem to vary with each case from relatively mild to severe loss of certain special abilities which seems to require the close cooperation of both cortexes. This is one of the reasons that Dr. Bogen does not recommend the operation to most persons, even if their epileptic seizures are severe. Like the removal of an entire hemisphere, it is strictly a last-resort measure.

I then asked Dr. Bogen if the operation could provide insight into mental illness, particularly schizophrenia. He admitted to some speculations. For example, the possible immanence of two centers of consciousness does have bearing on psychopathology – it is conceivable that the subjective agony of schizophrenia might be somewhat alleviated by a split-brain operation. The patient – or at least the consciousness in the dominant part of his brain – might be freed from the feeling of ambivalence that often cripples persons with this disease, rendering them incapable of decisive action – an ambivalence which may be the result of a conflict of the wills. But Dr. Bogen *emphatically does not recommend surgery as a ready solution for the treatment of mental illness.*

Some of the after-effects of surgery, such as the patients' loss of certain aptitudes, has led Dr. Bogen to formulate another interesting theory. He is convinced that "the other side of the brain," the hemisphere lacking verbal ability, may contribute to the creative consciousness.

"After the operation, certain losses and gains take place. The dominant side seems to lose the ability to think visually, while the minor hemisphere loses the ability to think verbally." This is evidenced by experiments in which the dominant side showed it was unable to copy geometric patterns accurately, while the other side no longer could write words although it copying of patterns was accurate. Dr. Bogen concludes, "Although the operation has confirmed the existence of two distinct individuals with complementary aptitudes, one verbal, one pictorial, the whole man, the patient, has lost some of his former ability to do both with each side of his body."

At the end of our interview, Dr. Bogen put me in touch with Dr. Philip Vogel, Chief Surgeon, who had been out of the country. Dr. Vogel underscored what others had said and added that "cerebral commissurotomy has been predominantly successful and appears to have a continuing place in the treatment of certain *selected* cases of epilepsy."

Next on my list was Dr. Bogen's patient, W.J., the first man to undergo surgery, who lives with his wife in the Southern-California area. W.J. sustained brain injuries leading to epilepsy during World War II. This makes him an atypical commissurotomy patient. Due to the fact that his brain damage occurred at the age of thirty, he is relatively free from the developmental scars of social adjustment so common in those who suffer medical handicaps in childhood.

W.J. looks just like any other partially-disabled veteran (he has other physical problems not connected with the operation). No one would know, off-hand, that only one side of his brain is conversing His other side usually just goes along for the ride, for it too knows itself to be W.J.

W.J.-major does not feel aware that there is another consciousness coexisting in him – he complains of a "dullness" in his left side. He simply regards himself as a whole person with different aspects. It is likely that W.J.-minor has pretty much the same attitude toward his whole self. As for W.J.'s wife – she notices no significant change.  He is still the same man she fell in love with and married over thirty years ago.


What makes the *whole man* ?

The split-brain phenomenon struck me as confirming philosophical intuitions already prevalent:  man *is* a social animal, even toward himself – he gets along with himself because information exchange – physical communication – is the basic feature of organic function.  In his daily life the countless sharings between the two halves of his brain, through exterior subliminal "cues," serve as unifying factors that permit us to say he is still one person, although he may possess two centers of awareness.  The degree and quality of information exchange between all the aspects of the self, all the levels of organic interaction, seems to be what really delineates the person – the whole man – who is extended in space and time far beyond the mere *feeling* that he is a consciousness.

My interview with Dr. Sperry mostly involved "shop-talk" in the philosophy of science, all of which seems too idiomatic to relate.  The full significance of his discovery may be destined to remain confined to professional journals, yet perhaps a small point can be made here:

As a member of the behavioral school in psychology, Dr. Sperry's redefinition of *consciousness* as  "a dynamic emergent property of cerebral excitation," represents a major revolution in theory which is bound to stir great controversy.  If accepted, it will lead to a revision in *Behaviorism* to include the phenomenon of Mind.  Up to now, the widespread application of knowledge obtained by the behavioral sciences to the healing of mental disease has been only partial and fragmented.  If an adequate and systematic account of the dynamics of consciousness could be given, by means of psychobiological descriptions of "mental states," it might lead to more direct and effective treatment of illnesses involving conscious processes.

Conscious experience would become inseparably tied to the material brain process with all its structural and physiological constraints.

But the conscious properties of brain function would encompass and transcend the details of neuro-physico-chemical events out of which they are built.  Just as the overall state of the organism determines the course and fate of its constituent cells and molecules, conscious properties of the brain would determine the flow pattern of subsequent neurophysiological events.

This proposal may be said to place *Mind* over *Matter*, but not as any disembodied or supernatural agent.

We would of course have to abandon our view of mind as something independent of the body – as a "ghost in the machine" that survives death of the body.

Many will accept the split-brain phenomenon as positive proof that no such *ghost* exists, that *consciousness* can cease to be – either when the body dies or when part of the brain dies such as happens in those injuries and afflictions that can turn a genius into a mental vegetable.

For those who choose to face this possibility, it raises the question of the supreme importance of the individual, here and now, not in some afterlife.

*ArtemisSmith* 1969

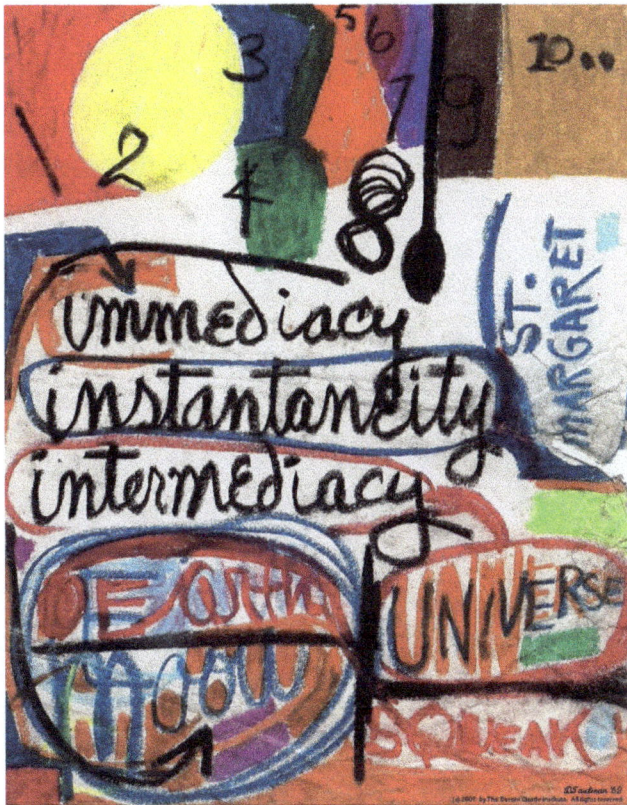

B. Taulman        crayon doodle        1964

# Who Am I ?  … and how can I live forever?

Which *I* is asking ?
How do I program a stem cell to *Become Me* ?
Do I want to become *Just-Me* or, *Someone Better-than-Me* ?
Do I want to remain the *Me* I have *at-this-point-in-time Become* ?
How many of *My* memories do I want to keep ?

The more I ask these questions, the more I realize that there is very little of *Me* that doesn't already belong to *Someone Else.*

Because all *Names* are not *Particulars* but *Universals,*
It follows that we are merely *ergodic* sources
                                    communicating in a *stochastic* field.
Our own signals are thrown back to us
                                    ever-changing our own configurations.
We recognize ourselves only through the substitution of indiscernibles.
Meanwhile the entire field is altered by this exchange.
Such is the pattern of *entropy*
                        and *time* is wholly ad hoc and context-dependent.

But the entire field bit by bit comes to reflect Me
Until My Silence creates a Void, filled by Other Voices.
I know this because phrases I spoke long ago have flowed back to me
In the tidal exchange of discourse.
And with each wave, the flotsam increases.
I am everywhere, touching everything until my discourse stops.

**Then is My Silence TERRIBLE,**
              **My Absence, the CRACKING of Your World.**

This is how Bereavement *IS* Time's Arrow though Indiscernibles persist.

*From "PteroDARKtyl Notes"  ArtemisSmith* 1957-2015

# 5. Toward a Logical Model of Conscious Behavior (lecture abstract 1970)

The objective of this course is to explore the possibility of constructing an adequate model for information exchange of the human central nervous system by taking an interdisciplinary approach to the description of the phenomenon of consciousness. Current issues in the philosophy of science in particular may be adapted to provide avenues of approach to an old problem.

Current fashion sees the description of a phenomenon to be the job of the scientist, while the task of evaluating the adequacy of the description is relegated to the philosopher of science. However the traditional problem of defining and understanding what is meant by the phrase "I am conscious" has heretofore fallen into philosophical hands, largely due to the scientist's reluctance to study what has not been deemed intersubjectively observable and more properly the subject of metaphysical and theological study.

Recently however some psychobiologists have taken the stand that the phenomenon of consciousness has epistemological relevance to the complete understanding of the functions of the human central nervous system. Research on alterations in the quality of consciousness as a function of alterations in CNS-pathways of activity have been carried on, notably, at the California Institute of Technology under R.W. Sperry, whose work on the split brain in man as forced a reassessment of the traditional concept of mind. This lecture series was compiled after conversations with the Sperry research team as well as other neurophysiological and cybernetic researchers in the area of Cal-Tech.

From the standpoint of the philosopher, many metaphysical theories accounting for consciousness have been put forth. The one most compatible with modern scientific advancement is that proposed by the scientific realists, who hold the contingent identity theory of mind and brain. Under this theory, an event-in-consciousness, more usually referred to as a "mental occurrence," is contingently identical to some neurophysiological occurrence in the brain. Thus some physiological event, $p$, is held to be the physical cause of some mental event, $q$. Yet the sentence, $|...p...|$ of some physiological theory $Tp$ has no logical connection to the sentence $|...q...|$ expressing the mental event in a natural language – since it is impossible to completely reduce one sentence to the other without loss of meaning.

However the scientist will find the scientific realist's proposal too abstract to serve the descriptive needs of cybernetic theory, for what is sought is some hypothetico-deductive neurophysiological theory of conscious behavior which renders the innocuous material implication [if $p$ the $q$] into the relation of strict logical entailment [ $p=>q$ ] that has the character of a law.

The problem for the model maker thus reverts to the problem of constructing a logical model for CNS-activity which has as its logical product a sentence in a natural language such as "I am conscious."

The additional problem, wholly in the realm of philosophy, consists in showing how such an utterance can be both true and significant, in that it does not distort common-sense intuitions of what it means to say, "I am conscious."

The tentative hypothesis put forth here as a possible explication of the concept of consciousness that will serve the needs both of the scientist and the philosopher, is thus the following:

### 1. consciousness
⇛ def. an aggregate of CNS-messages, either overt or covert, coded in social signs, either verbal or nonverbal, all of which have linguistic functions.

DISCUSSION: under this formulation, the following expressions lend themselves to a precise analysis

Consciousness is consciousness
> ⇛ def. an aggregate is an aggregate of a certain kind.

Consciousness is self-consciousness
> ⇛ def. an aggregate is self-identical (a contingent proposition which is false when the contents of an aggregate change).

Consciousness is conscious
> ⇛ def. an aggregate is aggregated according to certain laws.

Consciousness is self-conscious
> ⇛ def. an aggregate is aggregated precisely as itself (a contingent proposition which is false when the relations between the contents of an aggregate change).

## 2.a. **unit of consciousness**

∃ def. a CNS-message is such an aggregate, logically independent from all other units, past, present or future, but capable of being causally connected to other units by scientific methods of prediction.

(i.e., within a stream-of-consciousness sampling, such a unit is a fixed point which is not an indivisible, but an undivided; thus units of consciousness may be large or small, and their verbal reports may be studied by the researcher through the application of various laboratory techniques of indirect observation with the same kind of precision that we observe other indirectly observable phenomena.)

## 2.b. **logical status of a unit of consciousness**

∃ def. an ejaculatory utterance reporting a metatheoretical confirmation of the truth of a performative statement.

DISCUSSION: under this bridge-law formulation, which makes it possible for us to present a logical model applicable to the scientific prediction of behavioral connections between units within the aggregate, the following sentences lend themselves to a precise analysis

"I have a pain!"
    ∃ "[|It is true $_{ti+y}$…it is true $_{ti+1}$| 'hurting!' $_{ti}$ ]"
"I am experiencing a red sensum!"
    ∃ "[|It is true $_{ti+y}$…it is true $_{ti+1}$| 'red-ing!' $_{ti}$ ]"

which seems to satisfy the intuitive demand that the proposition be true only if the corresponding experience actually occurs in consciousness.

But whether this explication does indeed reflect the intuitive content of the ordinary-language concept of consciousness requires more than its substitutability in all cases. In the first place, precisely what is meant by "metatheoretical confirmation" in this instance itself requires explication in terms of offering some logical model for a CNS-phase leading to a conscious utterance of the type envisioned. Moreover, such a model should be adequate adequate to account for certain types of organismic behavior characteristic of human conscious activity – such as creative intelligence, pathological behavior, and the introspectionist's report of the ineffability of his stream-of-consciousness which seems always pregnant with the continuous present.

If certain recent conclusions in the philosophy of mind, and certain considerations now held to be key issues in the philosophy of science, are adapted to the solving of this problem – it may well be that the model we seek is already partially articulated and not so difficult to produce. It is the objective of this course to explore whether these fruitful ideas originating among philosophers might be adapted to serve the descriptive needs of the scientist.

I.   The first consideration deals with the problem of the status of "immediate impressions," a phrase primarily associated with Hume's contention that all our ideas of the external world arise out of and are combinations of strong impressions, each of which is a logically-isolated, independent particular.

So thorough was Hume's skepticism in this respect that it led him to the frank admission that even the concept of the *self* could not be considered an immediate impression, but rather an idea created by the mind which ordered its strong impressions according to some rule.

Hume's position was further articulated by Kant who held that the "I" of the Cartesian cogito was not an immediate intuition but rather reflected the transcendental unity of apperception as rendering consciousness of the present moment as *consciousness-for-some-observer.*

Telescoping further back in time, we come to a closely-related problem having to do with the logical status of impressions in Aristotle's contention, in the *Posterior Analytics, II,9,* that the logical particular cannot be spoken of except as it falls under its logical universal;  the argument for this is simple, and finds itself closely paralleled in Wittgenstein's modern destruction of the notion of a strictly private language in his *Philosophical Investigations.*

According to Wttgenstein (and Aristotle), let us suppose that someone has an impression, and writes down a sign naming it;  he could keep this kind of activity going on indefinitely, but then it would not be what we would call a *naming* activity, for the object of assigning a name to a thing is to recognize it as the same individual in the future – and if all our impressions are isolated, independent particulars, we possess no criterion for the reidentification of individual impressions.

The conclusion to be drawn from this argument is thus that all uses of words, including the simplest one of naming or denoting present-tense occurrences of particulars, involves the application of concepts which, rather than naively pointing to things in the world in a simple object-name correlation, catch whatever particulars in the immediate environment happen to satisfy the requirements of the special language-game being played.

This applies even to so-called atomic sense impressions such as *redness* which, in the first place, are not simple since the simplest impression of *redness* involves extension as well as color, hence is not simple, and moreover the notion of *redness* denotes a class of red impressions whose upper and lower bounds are not even clearly delineated in intuition (e.g., it makes sense to be undecided whether a particular sensation is red or brown).

The upshot of this telescoping back and forth in time, in the history of philosophy, is to gain support for the following proposal:

> If it is true (and the general agreement between philosophers supports this view) that no verbal sign denotes one particular exclusively, but only a class of particulars of a kind, then any meaningful utterance, such as the utterance "I" in the phrase, "I am conscious," is eliminable in favor of a description.

This is the subtle point of Russell's *Theory of Descriptions*:

> The sign "I" is a pronoun, equivalent to some expression such as, "this person," which is a logically proper name or denotation, and logically proper names are eliminable in favor of descriptions such as, "the individual $x$ at spacetime location $ywzt$" to which the predicate, "is conscious" may be affixed.

> (It is interesting to note that under this formulation and according to the definition of a "unit of consciousness" proposed, all propositions of self-reference become decidable under one or another logical strategy.)

The relevance to the behaviorist of this conceptual clarification of the logical status of the utterance, "I," should be evident – since it establishes the eliminability of first-person utterances in favor of equivalent expressions in the third person form, thereby doing away with the superstition that there are any expressions which, due solely to their grammatical form, denote a privileged and inaccessible experience.

That conscious experience is both private and inaccessible is not being denied by the above considerations – what is being denied is that its inaccessibility results from the fact that statements in the first person are of a *different logical type* than their counterparts in the third person. The inaccessibility of the conscious experience becomes thus grounded only in the obvious fact that their I, in reporting my inner states, receive my information and make my judgments according to a different set of confirmation procedures of a *physical* type than the confirmation procedures of the behaviorist whose measuring instruments are of a different *physical* type than those employed by my central nervous system.

And just as it is possible for me to be mistaken about where I have a pain (e.g., in a leg that may have been amputated), my own confirmations of my inner states are theoretical, and by no means infallible. While in most instances a report of my own inner states reflects a very high degree of confirmation, it is still possible for me to be mistaken, or to change my mind from moment to moment, according to the operations of CNS-information processing being performed.

Accepting the foregoing analysis makes possible the articulation of a model of conscious behavior which correctly reflects the result of increasing empirical evidence supporting the view that alterations of the quality of conscious behavior is the direct result of alterations in pathways of CNS-information processing (e.g., changes either in brain chemistry or the normal firing pattern of neurons – the most glaring examples of this being the Sperry split-brain phenomenon, the Penfield electrode study of the cortex, recent success in the psychobiological approach to treating psychoses, and the LSD tragedies of the 1960's).

II. If the above is acceptable, then it makes sense to propose that the problem of giving an adequate explication of conscious behavior can best be approached by offering a model which closely parallels the confirmation procedures of higher-order intellectual activity, such as exemplified in the theory-confirmation procedures of the natural sciences. Indeed, it is generally accepted that scientific reasoning is an extension of the same kind of reasoning underlying human individual intelligent activity. Conversely, might it not be possible that, by studying the behavior of the scientist, we might learn something about the behavior of the mechanism of intelligence in general?

The logic of decision and the logic of scientific discovery do properly belong to learning theory, and our two proposals for an explicans for a "unit of consciousness" were formulated with precisely this strategy in mind.

Talking about a "translation of a translation" of a "metatheoretical confirmation" raises approximately the same kinds of issues and problems dominating modern discussions in the philosophy of science, and demands very similar solutions. Two problems in particular, the problem of *radical translation*,

*translation*, and the problem of *choice between conflicting theories* ranging over the same observational domain, seem specially relevant.

(To these may be added a third, formulated by Nelson Goodman as *the new problem of induction* - the problem of just what is to count as a corroborating instance of an inductive hypothesis. I have set Goodman's problem apart from the others because I believe it can be shown to rest on a mistake: for Goodman seems to assume, perhaps only for the sake of showing its untenability, that what is "blue" and "green" and "grue" are immediately recognizable primitive sense qualities whereas, according to our thesis, even such qualities are not simple and are eliminable in favor of descriptions; nevertheless, the problem of just what constitutes a *natural kind* and what constitutes the reidentification of particulars that fall under it, is a problem that an adequate model of conscious behavior should solve.)

The problem of *radical translation*, first propounded by W.V.O. Quine in *Word and Object*, rests on the generally accepted modern empiricist assumption, germanelly related to what we have been discussing, that no description can function entirely in isolation but only within a system of descriptions, otherwise referred to as a *postulate system*. This being the case, it follows that the world can be described in an infinite number of ways, and that each observer in the world must approach it somewhat cryptographically, by putting forth linguistic hypotheses which catch or do not catch chunks of the world in ways that agree with the linguistic behavior of other observers.

Communication between observers thus proceeds by means of behavioral agreement, or *stimulus synonymies of linguistic signals*, rather than some internal shared semantic meanings that observers hold in common. The result is that each observer may have his own universe of private theoretical objects and private theoretical meanings and can never fully verify, on the level of stimulus synonymies, that another observer indeed shares the same "objects" in his private universe of discourse.

Between persons of a locale, whose shared linguistic habits are reinforced by a common lexicon and frequent message-exchange, variations in the meaning of social signs may be so slight a to be insignificant in most contexts. But as geographical distances increase, as well as differences in syntax, values, and other social objects, the problem of adequate translation also increases; *radical translation*, in any case − so Quine's theory states − is never reached.

Quine's stand is controversial and by no means generally accepted. However the notion of the impossibility of *radical translation* in natural languages has an extremely attractive feature applicable to our model of consciousness. If in finite systems of communication exchange *radical translation* is physically impossible, then might not the ineffability of the stream-of-consciousness be couched in precisely the failure, on the part of the CNS-information feedback network, to exactly duplicate, from phase to phase, the precise content of a previous message?

In other words, might the apparent incompleteness of verbalizations of conscious experience, the sense always that what is reported reflects a normalization of a message with much richer content than what can be uttered at any one time, rest in the brain's physical incapability to reverse time's arrow through *radical translation* ? Is there solipsism, not only relative to the whole brain, but within the brain among the various message-relay functions it contains?

If *radical translation* in a physical system of information exchange is impossible, this has the following consequence:

> The functions of the brain do not reflect a hierarchy of languages logically reducible to a common basis of primitive signals.

> Another way of putting this is to note that − between each phase of message-relay activity − only causal, and never logical, relationships hold. Similarities between behavioral acts proceeds via likenesses in stimulus chains, not equivalences or repetitions of logical configurations.

This precludes any linear sense to the phrase "metatheoretical confirmation" associated with our explication, such as is given in the Carnapian model of an extensional metalanguage in *Meaning and Necessity.* Rather, a Quinean (i.e., a probabilistic multi-theory *ontological relativity*) approach to the problem of theory confirmation seems more feasible and was indeed proposed by Kuhn. But the main difficulty with the Kuhnian *theory of paradigms* is that it too renders the notion of a common observation language between scientific disciplines wholly meaningless − yet when extended to the private observation language of conscious introspection, this seems counterintuitive.

It does make sense to ask, "Is this the same pain I had yesterday?" or, "Is this the same object I held in my hand a moment ago?"

While it is true that objects become, according to the Quinean model, merely thicknesses in the immediate fields of stimulus synonymies (i.e., statistical accumulations of behavioral responses to stimuli, as the psychologist already refers to them) this is insufficient by itself to account for the regularities of objective behavior which are evidenced by our ability to recognize, from moment to moment, a common world of common objects consciously persisting in time, despite the very wide variety of stimuli that evoke our like response at each moment of our perceiving and conceiving.

Is there some scientific middle ground between the hard form of Carnapian realism against which the Quinean/Kuhnian behavioral complexes appear as mere conventionalist strategies for the purpose of mirroring reality from the only coordinates accessible to the spatiotemporally limited observer?

What if the symbolic product of a chain of CNS-translation involving y-levels of stimulus meanings (the quantity of y determined by the experimenter) were not seen merely as containing information about what has gone before, but also to contain information about future strategies of confirmation, would this not ground objectivity in the question of *what the observer can be certain about the observer*, rather than what is observed?

Such a strategy avoids an ontological commitment to any real, fixed world beyond the possibility of experience by confining regularities to logical constructs alone, and not to the physical mechanisms which produce them, thus following in the Kantian tradition.

Further, applying the Leibnizian notion of logical compossibility to finite and small ranges of alternate observer-bound descriptions of the universe may not yield *Universal Truth* but does help us rank theories (as well as perceptions in the stream-of-consciousness) in a series, in terms of how much predictive observational content they contain, relative to each other, at unique parametric spacetime coordinates more commonly referred to as 'crucial experiments'.

The problem of presenting an adequate model for conscious behavior has its roots in learning theory. Learning in humans is presently seen as largely an extension of biological adaptive processes that may proceed by stimulus-response rote reinforcement in progressive stages of increasing complexity. Intelligent behavior is roughly viewed as both imprinted and habitual, the result of lower-level habitual/genetic behavior. But this model is highly inadequate for it commits us to a view of CNS-activity which is far too automatic and continguous with the robotic behavior of a highly-complex but insentient thinking machine.

However, when CNS-activity is viewed as *back-and-forth dialogue between a community* of lower order insentient thinking machines (as first proposed by Hilary Putnam) the immediacy of self-consciousness may be viewed only as an illusion. The range of the kind of illusion predicted to take place may further be determined by the application of Godel's technique used to test the incompleteness of axiomatic systems in logic.

Let us begin here.

*ArtemisSmith* 1970

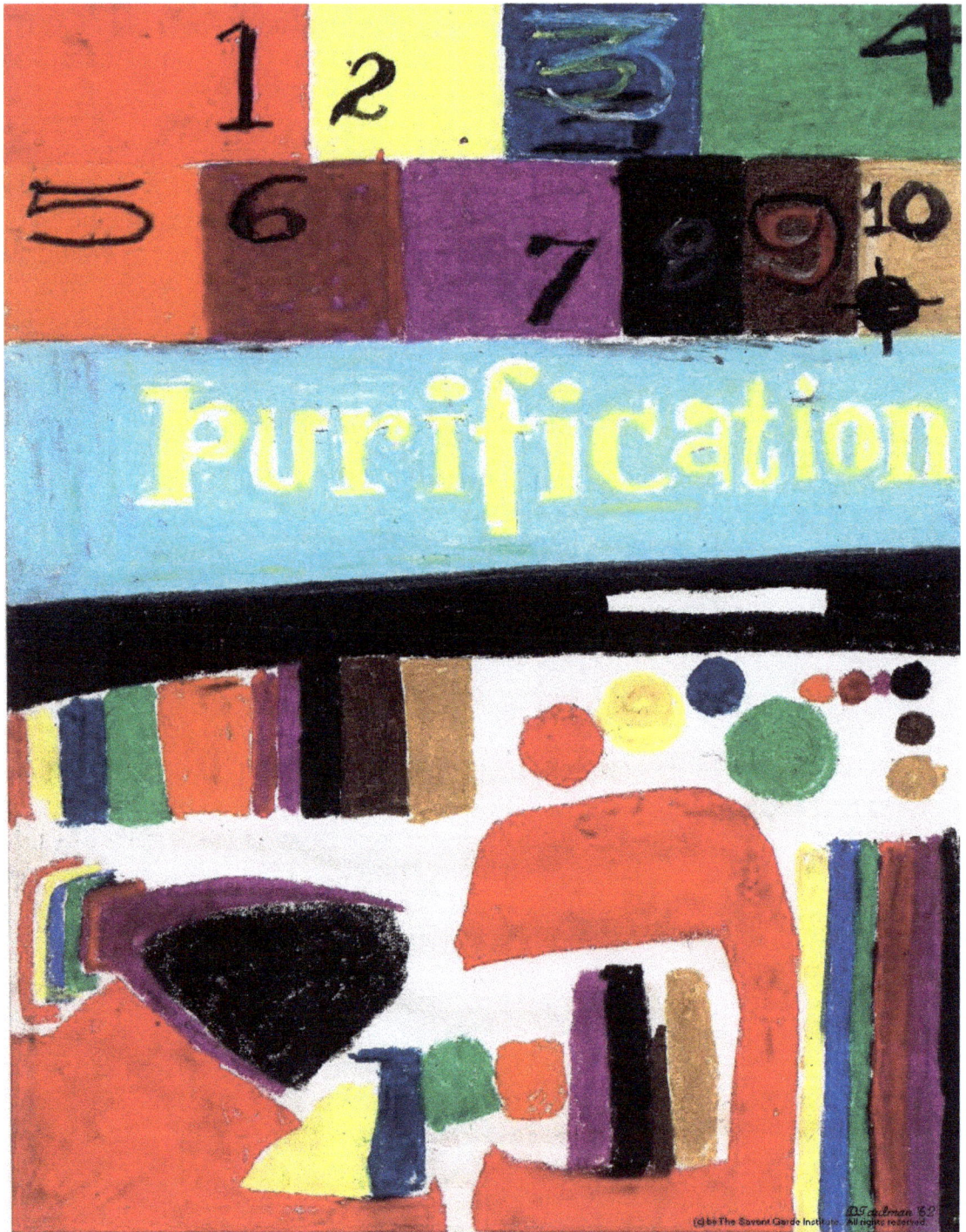

B.Taulman  crayon layout  1965

# 6. On Simulating <"I am Conscious!">=T
## ("A Cybernetic Model of Conscious Behavior from a Multi-Media Artist)

## Can "Consciousness(!)" be simulated?

**can a computer be programmed for "Consciousness(!)", or must such a physical unit for information exchange be strictly biological?**

My methodological decisions for proceeding to answer such a question entail, as a matter of personal taste, the rejection of vitalism, dualism, idealism, and any recourse to the notion of 'nomological danglers' which might help to evade the engineering question of "Consciousness(!)" programming.

I will attempt to describe consciousness in wholly epistemological terms which will leave little doubt to the information scientist that the phenomenon has been wholly accounted for in information theory terms.

An explication of the meaning of "I am conscious(!)" is thus the goal of this investigation.

A linguistic clarification of a term is, in the final analysis, the only warrant that a term has been fully defined within some central theory.

Especially in the case of "Consciousness(!)", construed as something private, nontransferable, a black-box event when purported to occur in others than ourselves - a linguistic clarification can be the only explanation, since all that is tangible about the phenomenon seems to be contained in language, and inspected by language; and philosophy is the discipline that ultimately studies consciousness qua "Consciousness(!)".

This is the direction in which, I think, the modern poet's best friend, Ludwig Wittgenstein, was headed, from *The Blue and Brown Books* to *The Philosophical Investigations*. My own investigation carries a little further what I believe to be sitting in front of everyone's philosophical nose today, as a result of Wittgenstein's analyses.

# 1. That pictures and descriptions are one and the same thing.

I see Wittgenstein's main point as having been that whatever exists, is "real" only to the extent that it can be "pictured" by some language; if we cannot speak in some way about something, we are forced to remain silent - a truism, yet we must remember that not all communication proceeds by way of vocal chords. Pointing to a thing is also speaking about it, for much more is assumed in the pointing than the "simple" act of pointing. Pointing is not a "logically simple" activity - it is communicative and depends upon a knowledge of the idiom (the language game) in which the pointing takes place; all pointing is learned behavior, must involve concepts.

But what if I turn inward and point to a thought inside my mind - isn't that kind of pointing "logically simple"?

According to Wittgenstein, who denied the sense of strictly "private" languages, the answer is no - no act of pointing is simple; all pointing assumes knowledge of a language game; in cybernetic terms, all pointing presupposes a program for the pointing activity.

Programs require a syntax and a semantical component; the latter requires a series of structural states determined by the architecture of the physical apparatus, and a context for its use - i.e., a task, or information-exchange environment.

It was my reading of Wittgenstein as hinting that all experience - both inward and outward - involves pointing, and that all pointing is complex and conceptual, that set me to thinking about a fruitful strategy for explicating "Consciousness(!)":

> If the whole of conscious experience might be shown to be a pointing activity, and no pointing activity might be shown to be "logically simple," then no part of conscious activity might be shown to be inaccessible to linguistic analysis, at least in principle; the "privacy" of my conscious experience would be grounded not on any kind of "simple" impressions or "ideas" I have spiritual access to, but on the mere logical and architectural facts of neural switching in my brain; my thoughts are private only because my nerve cells are connected to my integration centers and not anyone else's; if my switching patterns were simulated by another brain, it might be aware of my thoughts just as vividly as I am.

But before such a strategy can be gainfully pursued, a set of vaguely related problems must be briefly explored, for these still block the way to a complete description of "Consciousness(!)" in epistemological terms. I offer what follows only as a beginning to the search for a fully adequate plan for simulation.

## 2. An artist's notebook of sketchy attempts at a picture of "Consciousness(!)"

i.   On the hypothesis that all experience is complex (i.e., conceptual), hence in principle intersubjectively describable, what is the logical status of the content of a stream-of-consciousness?

> "Ideas" is the classical answer, and since we grant that graphic representations are a form of language, it is altogether too great a temptation to hold that "graphic utterances" form the logical content of a "Consciousness(!)" string. But such a simple explanation is inadequate, for how precisely do I "see" such images in my head without, ultimately, resulting to a form of dualism?

ii. Descriptions, furthermore, can be denied; message configurations can be rejected; theoretical constructs (proceeding from some central syntax of the brain, for example) are, even if only hypothetical, precisely reproducible.

> In contrast, the stuff of my awareness seems to have the character of the immediate, the undeniable, the irreproducible.

> If all my thoughts proceed from some central syntax in the brain, and are "graphic utterances" communicating information to other information-receiving centers in my brain, then my brain should be functioning in a much more deterministic manner, whereas I perceive a certain unpredictability about my future thoughts - a stochastic quality in my stream-of-consciousness, and a sense of time's arrow giving to each moment a fleeting uniqueness which, if I were a perfectly logical mind, I would not experience.

> A perfectly logical mind would keep reproducing eternal sentences, at least about those facts of inner experience that are not connected to perceptual input. Yet I, from moment to moment, have difficulty determining that a thought I had a moment ago is really the same thought I have now.

> Even analytic truths are judged true by me moment to moment only by appeal to the same rule, which I must, from moment to moment, recall.

iii. The stuff of my awareness - my "ideas" - carries an ontological quality which is not mere truth by derivation, but truth by immediate conviction despite a concomitant flow of contradiction.

> Being aware of something may be being aware of it as something of a kind, but it is also simultaneously being aware of it as being something of many different kinds, some of which are incompatible with the first.

(To point out, as Nelson Goodman does in *The Way the World Is*, that the way the world is seen is not the way the world is - is to point out that I see that the world I do see is not the only way I could see the world. The existence of a counterfactual possibility, in my awareness, gives that awareness a contradictory quality.)

### Dilemma:

> Logical descriptions of the world are supposed to be at least consistent - at best, complete. But the content of my awareness is ambiguous; if I thus hold that all conscious content is descriptive, I must also hold that all of my inward descriptions are equipollent - in an overall sense, intensionaly *meaningless*.

> But wouldn't this cancel out the sense of "awareness" associated with conscious experience? Moreover, how can I assert, from moment to moment, that I am the same consciousness experiencing the same world?

## iv. The objects in my world remain identical even though my descriptions conflict.

> It is not reality which is relative to my description - it is I who conform all my descriptions to reality.

> But if all my describing is equipollent, how is it possible for me to talk about (even when all the talking is by means of "graphic" terms) the same objects while using different intensional structures - i.e., different concepts or programs?

(In the philosophy of science, this problem is closely related to the problem of giving an adequate characterization of the correspondence of meaning between the terms of a scientific theory and their semiotic counterparts in a neutral observation language. P.K. Feyerabend has held, for example, that since a scientific theory - construed as a formalized, hypothetico-deductive system of concepts - inspects the world from its own particular viewpoint, and since rival theories have alternate intensional structures, no coincidence of intensional meanings among truly conflicting theories can ensue, even though terms used are semiotically identical, and such rival theories do not share a common ontology. Under this view, the notion of a common observation language for science is impossible, and all pointing to things in science becomes legitimate only within theories; all reality becomes, thus, relative to the observer, and purely conventional.)

My reality reflects an observer who is not merely bound to convention. My awareness is creative, and constantly leaps out of its own pictures of the world. Although this is not incompatible with the hypothesis that all my conscious activity proceeds from an underlying master program in which all the contradictoriness of consciousness is resolved, and each moment of my consciousness falls within a perfectly natural whole - this kind of hypothesis displeases me aesthetically. It implies that my mind is not really free and that the whole of my conscious experience is dictated by the rigid laws of classical logic embedded in unconscious processes of a dialectically determined type.

v. Can the alternate hypothesis - that "Consciousness(!)" is genuinely stochastic, proceeding from genuinely stochastic underlying processes in the brain - be maintained without resorting to a position of such extreme ontological relativity that both observer and world, from moment to moment, surrender identity?

(W.V.O. Quine (*Word and Object*) has attacked the problem of ontological relativity by holding that while it is true that sameness of intensional meaning cannot be maintained between two genuinely distinct languages, hence no radical translation achieved between them, there can still be extensional meanings which he terms "stimulus meanings" of semiotic notations which a community of observers, sharing like habits of response can attain. Thus their physical actions of signal-exchange have a kind of universal harmony (not necessarily due to the uniformity of nature but merely to the statistical accumulations of physical clusters of signal events) despite the radical solipsism of their intensional states.)

**This gets us closer to the information scientist's view of a communications network:**

> we have a network of sending-and-receiving mechanisms, each with its own language and set of programs, and each by a process of orthogonal development gradually adjusting itself, in a cryptographic manner, to a common program. Each unit scans the field, and alters itself accordingly.

**Two possibilities for reality are permitted according to this view:**

> (1) *either* reality is completely determined (in which case, eventually all the views will become one);

> (2) *or* reality is stochastic (in which case, all the physical processes within it, including the sending-receiving units themselves, are mere fleeting thicknesses in the flow of events, all language is fluid, and logical truth merely a temporary illusion).

Perverse as it may seem, as an artist I would like to hold the latter view and see whether, from such a state of affairs, a real world can still follow. If I can show that a real world can indeed follow from it, I will have shown that language in such a world does indeed mean something and that, if conscious strings are linguistic, consciousness is what I already know it to be - filled with meaning.

But meanings require the possibility of analytic truths. How is this possible in a world in which logical truths are not fixed entities?

A semantic theory by Jerry A. Fodor and Jerrold Katz points to a characterization of analytic truth in terms of linguistic behavior of respondents in an information-exchange network:

> analytic behavior is the tendency of respondents in a community to give synonymous response to the terms of a natural language with a probability approaching 1; synonymies listed in a lexicon form the empirical basis for the formulation of a semantic theory giving the intensional relations between all the signs in a natural language; since analytic meanings are least variant among all the meanings in a language, they determine the ontology for that language.

> (In information science terminology, analytic sentences are messages of lowest entropy. In contrast, of course, contradictory sentences may be termed messages of highest entropy.)

According to this model, a world of common objects may be maintained, approximately, ranging over some domain of space and time.

In such a world, information exchange can proceed, with a minimum of inaccuracy, long enough for real objects to remain more-or-less identical over an indefinite period. Moreover, the notion of logical truth in such a world is hardly mere fleeting illusion, since it reflects those types of linguistic behavior which are the least susceptible to alteration.

I can, therefore, thanks to Katz and Fodor, maintain my perverse view of reality, even if it turns out that they prefer seeing the world as a completely determined place.

## vi. What kind of world have I stepped into?

As Quine has pointed out (*Two Dogmas of Empiricism*), the classical notion of analytic (i.e., logical) truth depends on a prior knowledge for its application which for the empiricist, was only guaranteed by immediate intuition.

But immediate intuition, being simple, is indemonstrable, hence optional for each observer, and all intersubjective logical truth is conventional (i.e., learned through orthogonal development in a community). Moreover, logical truth in the sense of *analytic-in-L* is only demonstrable in artificial languages, since natural languages are inconsistent.

Furthermore, a natural language lexicon, which reports the analytic behavior of a community, is an empirical semantic theory based upon generalizations from past usage; while while it can be used to predict, within a range, the linguistic behavior of a community of respondents, it can give no insight into the ultimate layout of the real; and because natural languages are ambiguous, all analytic behavior is stochastic and held to physical reality only by the behavioral notion of stimulus-synonymy, which defies radical translation between the private languages of respondents.

The import of this last consideration is, for us, not only that (a) I am cut off from the rest of the community in terms of the solipsism of my intensional meanings, but that (b) every linguistic function in my own brain is cut off from every other linguistic function by the same rule. The only guaranteed sameness of meaning possible in such a model of mind must be wholly extensional - i.e., nonlinear - and dependent upon how many slicing operations my scansion apparatus can perform in the tracking of a signal, from one sampling to the next.

But this works out well for us when we consider that we recognize stimulus-synonymies between pictures-and-words as well as between pictures-and-pictures, and words-and-words. This kind of pattern recognition does permit me to claim that a word and a picture, or two pictures of the same word, are all descriptions of the "same" object - when the object is construed as beyond language, as the signal which is being tracked.

vii. But is it also adequate to account for my intuition of linearity (i.e., my intuition of logical derivation from premises to conclusion)? For although the overall configuration of my awareness is stochastic, it has clusters in it which are more predictable, more determined than the rest .

Are such patterns of linear behavior simply those architectural changes that my biological computing mechanism undergoes, in its orthogonal development, as the result of accumulations of more stimulus synonymies? (B.F. Skinner's behaviorism would seem to imply this.)

viii. But my awareness is creative:

I am able to recognize synonymies between pictures and words that I have never learned to correlate previously, even in entirely new contexts of action. This kind of behavior reflects transformational properties rather than mere operant conditioning of apparatus.

Katz and Fodor follow Chomsky in holding a transformational view of linguistic behavior; might this not be extended to the whole range of linguistic behavior, both graphic and verbal, and graphic-to-verbal, and verbal-to-graphic?

For example, there seems to be an isomorphic correspondence between all the pictures we can draw of geometric figures, and their algebraic notations (although the notations we use are sometimes only normalizations when such figures are extremely irregular and defy precise mathematical description).

Drawing or tracking a picture is one kind of behavior, fitting an algebraic notation to it is another; what language does the brain use to correlate the figure with the formula?

This is a case in which I engage in one kind of conceptual activity which is made to serve as a template for another kind of conceptual activity. In each case, I might be applying the same syntax, but because of the difference in the architecture of the apparatus which uses that syntax, there is a radical difference in the objects produced as the result of that activity.

**Here there may be a key to the qualitative difference I sense between my visual and my verbal awareness:**

I am aware that using my eyes and hands to communicate with feedback centers in my brain produces, even though I use the same rule, an entirely different set of consequences than the use of my verbal apparatus produces.

Such consequences are then correlated in the next round.

# 3. An artist's leap to a preliminary portrait of Consciousness(!)

Might not the identity between a word and a picture be couched in a verification procedure which the brain undergoes, to determine that the same rule is being employed in the production of the verbal and graphic messages?

If so, I am a step nearer to an explication of a conscious string, for consciousness is consciousness of a correspondence between pictures and words with all the other pictures and words in the attention field; and it is more than mere statement but judgment of that correspondence - i.e., an act carrying ontological commitment.

Let's try a Turing model.

Picture a machine that contains

(a)  a set of alternate receptors and communicators, using the same syntax.

(b)  a mechanism for orthogonal development, based upon first-level operant conditioning and second-level transformational response.

(c)  a nonlinear decision procedure for pattern recognition, proceeding epistemologically, via multiple hypotheses.

**A tentative characterization of a conscious string for such a machine might be:**

*the Nth-level confirmation of an ith-level truth-claim*.

The string is linguistic, an ejaculatory utterance from the brain which carries a performative statement:

"I am verifying! that I am verifying! that I am verifying! ... that ("...x...!") is True!"

The idea came to me while reading Hillary Putnam's paper, *Minds and Machines*. There, he uses the example of two Turing machines which scan each other's states and become utterly confused, after some rounds of information exchange, as to which machine is in which state.

For example: When I say, "I have a pain," do I mean my hand or my brain?

If I mean:   "I, the information-exchange network, have a pain,"

then the pain is no longer such a simple feeling; there is something decidedly linguistic about it, intersubjective, a message covertly couched in the third-person form rather than the immediacy of the first-person form in which it is outwardly expressed.

But what kind of a message? Surely no simple sentence such as "I have a pain" is sufficient information to be contained in a consciousness string.

If Machine A says to Machine B, "B has a pain,"

B should have a program for responsive action that verifies A's claim - it should be able to kick and scream and indulge in sophisticated strategies of pain-avoidance.

## A model like this will only work if:

(a) the programmed behavior is sufficiently coordinated and complex;

(b) the semantical component involves the mechanism in existential situations in which self and not-self are sufficiently clear and consistent concepts for the self-programming network;

(c) it is not linguistically absurd to hold that first-person truth-claims are of the same logical type as third-person truth-claims.

**The impossibility of (c) would void the whole object of our investigation and must, therefore, be investigated first.**

A quest for a logically-certain proof that "I" and "...x..." are logically equivalent would be self-defeating since the determination of a logical type falls into two categories;

(1) either the classification of two terms into one type is conventional, hence optional, or,

(2) there is some kind of essential relation between them, discovered in intuition

but the latter hypothesis is precisely what we are trying to destroy. The kind of linguistic fact we seek to establish is that the identity relation

$$"I" = "...x..." \text{ or } "it"$$

between two logically proper names (the subjects of a denotation) is contingent because not self-contradictory.


## Only an informal proof is possible:

An observation of my linguistic habits shows that my use of the exclamations "I hurt!" and "It hurts!" are sometimes equivalent.

I also readily identify myself as the subject of others' denotations when they refer to me as "you" and "she"; if there were a type difference between the pronouns, wouldn't I have a difficulty with others' use of the pronoun "I"?

The history of philosophy gives further corroboration to the view that the subject of an "I" denotation is conceptual rather than immediate. The Cartesian cogito was never offered as a proof for the existence of God as a simple fact of the mind (Descartes had to prove the existence of God before he could establish the integrity of the self as something existing apart from the dream of an "evil genius"); the most simple, basic truths that Descartes found in intuition were qualities existing in complex relations, and the self was not among these - was not an impression like redness or pain.

Hume tore apart the claim that the self was a simple impression.

Kant agreed with Hume.

Bertrand Russell gave his *Theory of Descriptions* which holds that all proper names (including logically proper names) are eliminable in favor of descriptions; the import import of this theory is that all things may be talked about in the third-person description which fits them. This means that the sentence, "I hurt." may be rewritten as "The individual, x, such that (some adequate description for locating x in space-time) ... is hurting."

But even if the "I" of the "I think" is conceptual, as we are arguing, does it follow that there are no simples whatsoever in our awareness - that the whole of it is fully descriptive of a lower-level occurrence?

The superstition still persists, if indeed it is only a superstition, although both fathers of philosophy, Plato and Aristotle, didn't think so.

Plato, in the *Theatetus*, tore apart an early version of logical atomism by pointing out that the wholes in our introspection cannot be fully reduced to a mere sum of their parts.

Aristotle, whose *Posterior Analytics* set the pace for scientific demonstration based upon intuited first principles, did not hold that the indemonstrable first principles were in any sense atomic; on the contrary, he offered a very sophisticated theory of perception which held that the world outside of us and the world within us are both parts of the same vitalistic process in which our powers for observing the world depend upon the assumption of a potentiality in the observer to see, and a potentiality in the observed to be seen - that is, in a very information-theory-like view of the special relation between signal-senders and signal-receivers.

## Among the moderns,

Russell, one of the fathers of Logical Atomism (the movement which preceded Logical Positivism and tried to isolate the simple qualities of introspection which Hume's phenomenalism took for granted), ended by admitting that while particulars are logically eliminable in favor of universals, universals are not eliminable in favor of particulars, since every meaningful utterance must contain at least one constituent and one component.

Wittgenstein, as previously noted, denied the existence of strictly private languages; his argument, though more eloquent, closely parallels the one used by Aristotle (*Post. An. II,9*):

if there were such things as particular names, the reasoning goes, then I would have to keep naming everything that happens in my awareness; the activity would go on indefinitely; but then the whole sense of assigning names to things would be lost altogether; we name things to recognize individuals when we see them again; names are universals - merely shorthand signs for descriptions.

To my knowledge, not even the continental intuitionists hold to a theory of simples in awareness. The undeniable intuitions they present are usually the relational complexes of classical (Kantian) space and time; but these are arbitrary since intuitions of non-Euclidean space-time, as well as paradoxes of class containment, are conceivable. Nor are the simple ideas of my own introspection truly indivisible, since even the sensation of redness in recollection is an impression which contains both extension (a spatial component) and a concept of what not-red is.

The subtle difference in the conflict of theories of knowledge between the (usually continental) proponents of a Leibnizian conceptualism and the (usually empiricist) proponents of a form of Hobbesian constructivism is paralleled, I believe, in the subtle shift of viewpoint of the Wittgenstein of the *Tractatus* to the Wittgenstein of the *Philosophical Investigations*: it is a movement from the intuitionist's belief that there are logical simples in language which can form the building blocks of all our deductive reasoning, and the constructivist's belief that all the simples in language are not indivisibles but only undivided starting points for our deductive reasoning - beginning anywhere, in any suburb of language, can be a precise beginning, depending on the descriptive job to be done; we build from what has gone before.

The model of conscious behavior I envision holds to this latter, constructivist view, seeing all of consciousness as fully filled with language, emanating from lower order processes of linguistic information exchange. At each level stand stimulus-meanings, facts of a physicalistic kind, describable in a neurophysiological language.

(Those who prefer may add that these physical relations reflect a transcendental order in things - but I don't have to accept this latter hypothesis since my view of a stochastic universe also provides a temporally-extended stable reality, and a choice between determinism and indeterminism is optional, beyond the limits of possible experience.)*

*[1984 addendum: Many persons reading the original of this work mistakenly assumed that my view of a stochastic universe in some way implied that nothing in such a universe could authentically be considered *Sacred*. This would be a misreading of the particular philosophy of religion accompanying the proposed new concept of mind. My own position, as both artist and philosopher, derived from the line of reasoning in this paper, is that no graven image - whether in thought or in speech - can be a simple representation of *The Sacred*. Hence miracles and direct expressions of faith are all neutral mental phenomena to be made subject to the same epistemological investigations that accompany the verification of any other utterance of the mind. If this view threatens the doctrine of any established religion - let it do so with impunity, as a religion in its own right.]

# 4. An artist's glimpse of the cybernetic model of mind:

Let us hypothesize that units of consciousness, whether large or small, are essential links in the chain of epistemological information-exchange in the central nervous system of a complex self-programming unit which has powers for action of a type involving multiple experimentation. Why should the emergence of consciousness in such a unit fulfill a particular epistemological need?

Only an answer to a question of this type can satisfy the scientist that consciousness is a genuine effect of natural causes. I believe the answer lies in the kinds of adaptational decisions made possible by the presence of conscious processes not made possible at any other level of cybernetic adaptational activity:

> I have in mind those acts of experimentation which involve creative problem-solving within existential contexts of a highly dynamic type - activities without which both organisms and machines very quickly deteriorate into mere ritual behavior (characterized by high redundance of patterns of action, high rigidity in the face of new situations - i.e., stimulus-analytic behavior carried to the point of empty tautology, lowest-entropy communication, informational incapsulation, logically rigid and paranoid behavior).

But neither are conscious processes wholly unpredictable - for it they were, they would not constitute an awareness of anything at all, for some underlying integrity of action is needed in order to preserve those perceptual parameters that fix an observer in a definite set of conceptual relations to a fixed observation field.

> Consciousness as a process maintains a homeostatic mean between extremes of rigidity and fragmentation, informational redundance and informational variegation.

But how precisely might conscious processes be maintaining such homeostasis? This is the question the engineer legitimately asks and, not being a mathematician, I cannot presume to offer more than a sketch of a model for the answer. The descriptive materials I will use are bits and pieces borrowed from symbolic logic and Leibniz's *Monadology*, reconstituted to apply to a local universe and a nonvitalistic, information-theory viewpoint:

> I see the conscious string as containing a hash-coded engram carrying information of two types - confirmatory and disconfirmatory, of the last round of sensori-motor experimentation activity; the product of the reception by lower-order processes of this conscious string is a new response, the next conscious ejaculation, of a logically-creative type in relation to what has gone before.

In logic, the term "creative" has a special application: it denotes those undecidable sentences of an incomplete postulate system which, when added to the primitives, do not affect its inner consistency but alter the set of sentences derivable from it; moreover, a "creative" definition is viewed as one that broadens the meaning of a term beyond what the simples of the system determine.

Analytic behavior is, ideally, absolutely noncreative;  in contrast, self-contradictory behavior is, ideally, absolutely creative - bearing a highest-entropy message;  to contradict a tautology is to reverse the informational entropy of that function which produces a specific signal within the class of signals constituting a hash-coded message string.

A priori schemes - conceptual networks - are traditionally viewed as networks of tautologies.  What if the hash-coded message in the conscious string assigns a value 0 for all tautologies posited by lower-order computational outputs; which lower-order messages would survive the event?

The logical product of a structural "clash" between all their inverse functions, surely, and - more importantly - all the programs which are neutral to the negation taking place since they are incomplete relative to the logical content of the conscious string being received as a signal.  (Such neutral programs are, in some sense, options, metaphysical posits.)

The programmer knows better than I the details of such a negative-feedback process; its essential character is adaptational, as I believe Norbert Wiener anticipated, and the kinds of message feedback configurations such a complex information network would engage in results in behavior of a logically creative type.

Suppose we view all the myriad conceptual programs of the mind as each providing a multivalued response to a signal contained in a conscious string (i.e., either assigning it a value of 1 or 0 or some value between 1 and 0 in terms of chemically-stored action potentials);

that is, suppose we view each conceptual program as a "theory" for which the signal functions either as a reinforcement or an inhibition or a neutral action potential;
then, the end-product of a chain of information exchange in response to this signal is some limit of feedback, R, which is a compromise - the best of all "compossible" configurations resulting from the field of conceptual systems at play;

and R, as a hash-coded message, feeds back to the lower-order processes as a set of signals, together with new input from inner and outer sense.

The above is a model for consciousness which falls under a certain type, extensible into higher-level models for scientific, artistic, and moral discovery. For the multiple-theory, multiple hypothesis approach which characterizes such epistemological activity can help us determine, nonlinearly and with optimum information retention, which theories to revise and which to discard in any observational domain. The physical economies of theory revision provide the criterion for garbage-disposal.

## Concluding remarks:

This model of consciousness, I believe, makes possible an account of both aesthetic and moral behavior as something more than mere conditioned response culturally-instilled.

By maintaining that consciousness works against excessive analytic behavior, and does so in an epistemological framework, acts which function as optimizations of observational probing are made genuinely acts of optimal adaptation.

Much in the classical tradition, I see moral awareness as proceeding from aesthetic awareness which is the result of a cultivation of those habits of sensori-motor adaptation which increase our powers for epistemological choice.

I see such awareness as fostered by the very opposite of rote teaching and operant conditioning; rational - epistemological - choice is the result of the preservation, through a liberal and diversified education, of all our powers of choosing between equipossible, equivalid alternatives.

*ArtemisSmith* 1972

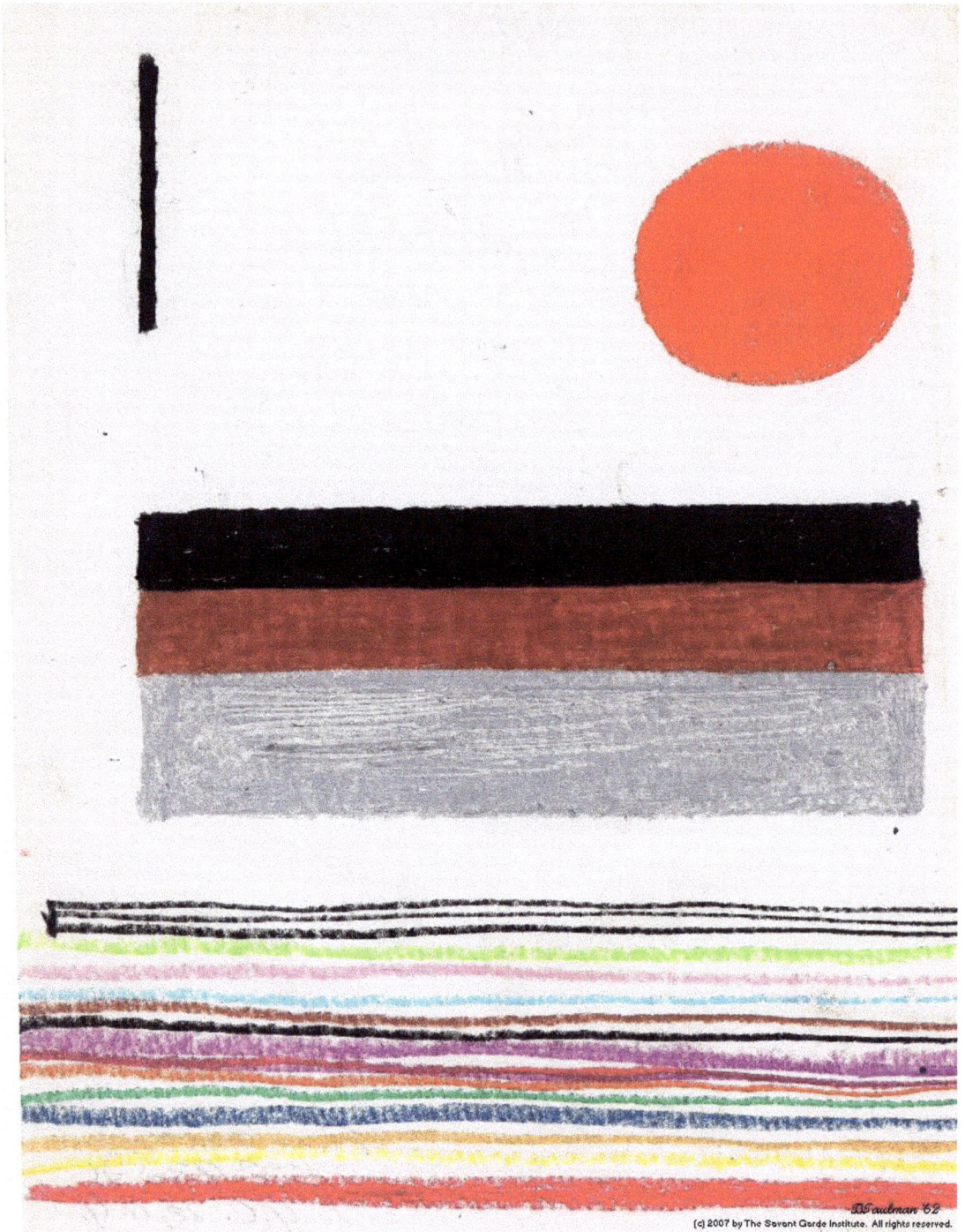

B. Taulman  "Somewhere Over the Rainbow"  1965

# 7. Toward a Scientific Explication of Synesthetic Phenomena through Kinesthetic Stimulation (its relevance to sexology)

## INTRODUCTION

What follows is part of a general trend to form and articulate a central theory of aesthetics from an information-science viewpoint.

Application of information-science concepts to neurophysiology, especially in the area of sensorimotor learning, has placed the study of kinesthetic behavior such as occurs in improvisational dance, as well as other movement phenomena including the enjoyment of sexual interplay, as basic to the study of aesthetics when viewed as an extension of human epistemological activity engaged in by the psychobiological system.

In particular, some recent successes in prosthesis for the blind through the use of a multimedia tactile-visual substitution system, in which kinesthetic response plays a key factor, would lead psychophysical researchers to new hypotheses about the status of 'phantom limb phenomena' of all kinds and, here specifically, the nature of mutual sexual gratification therefrom.

The central hypothesis of this view of mind and aesthetic experience (under which category higher-level human 'lovemaking' may be included) is entirely dependent upon tactile perception for its continued presence, and this perception cannot proceed without constant sensorimotor experimentation at-a-short-distance in real space and time.

Such existential experimentation, falling under the larger category of epistemological behavior, is an on-going information exchange process in which the quality of consciousness produced in the observer (i.e., including a state of orgasm) is directly determined by the kinds of sensorimotor experimental strategies available to the perceiver/communicator.

Such strategies proceed through kinesthetic feedback from the periphery, wherefore the phenomenon of spontaneous orgasm may be the outcome of an extension of such primary perceptual activity at the point where the agent or agents take 'joy' in the sheer act of interplay.

The presence of "completion" in perception may occur when perceiving becomes more than a pragmatic activity—when the entire organism engages in spontaneous creative interplay with the environment and acquires options for new percepts as a result of such increased sensorimotor activity that greatly extends the adaptational abilities of the perceiver resulting in a feeling of general 'freedom' and 'well-being'.

Some years ago [cf. *"ArtemisSmith's A Cybernetic Model of Conscious Behavior from a Multimedia Artist."* 1972 Masters' Thesis, CUNY: The City College.] the author first proposed the hypothesis that human consciousness was an extension of perceptual behavior at the point where such behavior becomes creative rather than merely pragmatic. It was seen as emerging from lower-level epistemological activity which, in the process of linguistic translation within all the chemico-neural languages of the psychobiological system, acquires the kind of aesthetic ambiguity present in metaphor, i.e., of a "metasporic" synaptic state.

This hypothesis rested heavily on earlier work in learning theory (Piaget, 1947, 1963) and cybernetics (Wiener, 1948, 1961), and the philosophical investigations of Wittgenstein and Quine; the latter specifically addressed the question of translation and objectification in behavioral semantic systems.

From a neurophysiological standpoint, the author's investigations into the nature of human consciousness came specifically as a reply to certain questions posed by later-Nobel-laureate R.W. Sperry, head of the split-brain research team at California Institute of Technology (Sperry, 1966, 1967, 1969, 1970), regarding mental causality and mind-body interaction.

In 1969, the author had occasion to inspect the experimental facilities at Cal-Tech and to interview split-brain researchers and patients. At that time, I discussed with Professor Sperry the possibility of providing a logical explication of the phenomenon of consciousness, in information science terms, that would meet the rigorous requirements of the non-dualist philosopher.

In 1972 I subsequently proposed and published such an explication. This rested heavily on the findings of the split-brain team that the quality of human consciousness depends upon which cortical aptitude centers play the most active roles in the experimentation-objectification process of perceiving.

In psychological terms, this is equivalent to the claim that our 'attention sets' or predispositions to perceive are the key factors in determining which objects in the perceptual field are actually noticed; further, that the parameters of observation, as fixed by our sensory apparatus, determine the physical limits of the perceptual field.

Thus, any phantom limb, whether it be a prosthetic retina or a mechanical hand or an artificial penis, determine the quality of the input and the physical limits of the perceptual field.

But the question of creativity in perception requires that we explain precisely how it is that 'attention sets' arise from which the spontaneous declarations of "I am conscious of *such and such …!*" arise.

Such ejaculatory utterances do not emanate solely from problem-solving behavior but reflect nonspecific responses to stimuli that Piaget termed the "play instinct"—*i.e.,* the tendency of the open system to engage in experimental activity for the sheer need to keep itself in a state of constant activity or else risk deteriorating into a rigid system. "Joy - immediacy" in perception is somehow related to this basic, open-system characteristic. The presence of this creative free-play, for the sake of maintaining maximum options for organismic adaptational function, is what distinguishes the open system from the closed system—the biosystem from the machine.

How the neurophysiological system leads to human consciousness may be parodied in the old game called "Russian Scandal." The game involves a group of persons sitting in a circle; the first player whispers some gossip in the adjacent person's ear, and the story is passed on to each person around the circle; when it reaches the last player, the story with all the distortions is told out loud; it is likely to be barely recognizable from the original.

So it is with the various centers of the brain—each in its own neurophysical language gives a message to some other center. At some point, the transformation of this message comes to be expressed either in spoken language or body behavior—that transformation, with all its distortions, is what appears in the ejaculatory immediacy called *Consciousness* and its overt declaration is what determines which parts of the perceptual field are most confirmatory of future expectations of perception—*i.e.,* the next 'attention set'.

Movement is vital to human perception; without it, consciousness comes to be depressed and even eliminated. As was discovered very early in Pavlovian experiments involving the orienting reflex, the eye that is fixed upon an object and not permitted to utilize its oculomotor reflexes soon becomes unable to see; the ear that is exposed to the same tone for a length of time develops a deafness to that tone. The more perceptual experiences are associated with an object, the more vivid that object becomes. In the aesthetic experience, which includes the human sexual experience, we come to be acquainted with objects, situations, persons, in ways that our ordinary perceptual apparatus would not normally perceive; this too is movement, of a higher-order kind.

Confirmation of such a view of the entirely linguistic nature of *Consciousness*, only barely outlined here, will come from areas of science concerned with simulating higher-level conscious experience either in machines or in humans utilizing bionic replacements for lost or nonfunctioning sensorimotor apparatus—*i.e.,* as in varying kinds of prostheses.

The term prosthesis is most often associated with the crude replacement of limbs, but eyeglasses and hearing aids are also prosthetic equipment, as are artificial kidneys and pacemakers.

That eyeglasses may enhance the quality of sight is of course a truism, but the true aim of visual prosthesis is to mimic the retina or other site of visual processing in such a manner as to make it possible for a blind person to "see" precisely as a normal person.

To do this, it is not enough simply to supply an alternate source of information assimilation at-a-distance, such as might be accomplished through a cane or auditory scanning device; rather, the aim of such prosthesis is to create an "eye" that actually produces images directly to the brain as the natural organ does - where the image received is hooked up to the central nervous system in such a way as it can appear as an actual mental image; proof that this kind of prosthesis is possible provides a vastly significant advance in the theory of mind-brain interaction.

Below follows an account of a remarkable success in achieving such a visual-substitution system that points inescapably to the validity of the information science concept of mind, and its grounding upon kinesthetic behavior, as a prerequisite for the emergence of human consciousness of all kinds.

The prosthesis referred to is called The Tactile Visual Substitution System (TVSS) and it was developed in the late 1960's at Pacific Medical Center, San Francisco, where this research is still continuing. Principal researchers are P. Bach-y-Rita and C.C. Collins of the Center's Institute of Medical Sciences.

In the initial experiment, six blind persons, five of whom had been blind since birth, and six normal-sighted persons functioning as controls, were provided with a tactile analogy of a retina. The skin of the patient's back was chosen as the tactile surface and a grid was constructed on which 400 vibrating points capable of electromechanical activation were laid at ½-inch intervals; this grid was connected to an analog computer which digitized geometrical information received through a television camera, so as to permit the subject to receive television pictures in the form of vibratory information on their skin; the apparatus was set into a dental chair in which the subject sat, stripped to the waist.

But the simulation of sight goes far beyond the provision of a substitute retina. The oculomotor reflexes, which move and focus the eyeball, play a vital role in sight, through kinesthetic feedback to the brain; in fact, sight is not possible without such constant oculomotor activity. Consequently, the researchers equipped the television camera with a zoom lens for alternate focusing and set the camera on a flexible tripod which the patient was permitted to manipulate himself, thereby permitting his entire body to function kinesthetically in a manner approximating oculomotor activity.

After being introduced to the mechanics of the system, subjects were taught to discriminate first between various geometrical lines and shapes, and then their combinations including three-dimensional forms. After approximately one hour of such training, they were introduced to a "vocabulary" of 25 ordinary objects, such as chairs, cups, telephones. After less than ten hours of training, recognition time for these objects fell to 20 sec., and recognition time for new objects which the subjects had not been trained to *see* also fell markedly; this speed in recognition was directly dependent, in most cases, on the subject's ability to manipulate the television apparatus himself rather than through an intermediary, thus firmly establishing the hypothesis that kinesthetic feedback plays an important part in visual perception.

What was even more startling, however, was that subjects reported the locus of visual perception to be in front of them, where their eyes are, rather than on the skin of their back where the stimuli were being received. Not only this, but blind subjects were able to discover distinctly visual concepts, such as perspective, shadows, shape distortion as a function of viewpoint, and apparent change in size as a function of distance; moreover, they could recognize objects, letters, persons, and moving stimuli even from the barest cues—such as the cord of a telephone or the handle of a cup! And all of these stimuli were subjectively interpreted as visual, by both blind and the nonblind control subjects!


One of the key questions raised by the experiment was why an area of the skin on the back of a person—not a very sensitive area at that—should work as well as a more sensitive one, such as a hand. The answer, still then speculative, speculative, was that most of what goes on in perception is the work of central structures of the brain which can modify and amplify even the most sparse peripheral input by linking it to a multitude of already-learned responses. Thus the important part of perceiving was not the input from the periphery, but the body's own record of motor adjustments to outward cues—the richness of the perceptual experience being directly correlated to the amount of freedom for sensorimotor experimentation available to the perceiver—how flexible was the television viewing apparatus, how finely could it be adjusted or shifted in space—that is, how closely could it mimic the motor operations regularly performed by the muscles of the eye in sighted subjects.

Questions about the quality of perception were then reduced precisely to questions about the quantity and pattern of information exchange, such patterns being determined by the kinds of motor operations permitted the perceiver.

Motor operations functioned as hypotheses in a bioepistemological experimental process, providing the spatiotemporal parameters for prescientific observation. *Seeing* was thus regarded as continuous with *learning* and *concept formation.*


## LANGUAGE AND EPISTEMOLOGY

An epistemological activity is perforce a behavioral/linguistic process, for it proceeds by way of a syntax and rules for transformation and produces, for each signal input, a set of alternate analytical informational parameters for the next round of synthetic experimentation. Natural language, as a pattern of sound notations, is only an analogue of this more primitive neuronal information-exchange process and the very expression of natural language is in the topological *graphic language* of peripheral sensory input. A mathematical model for storage and retrieval of information in the neural network has been offered by a number of researchers, notably Sebestyen (1962), and Zeeman (1964), which has direct application to Aristotelian word hierarchies and Boolean set theory, which in turn led themselves to natural language semantic structures as modeled by Katz and Fodor (1964). Space does not permit in-depth analysis of these issues here, however they rely on earlier work by Godel on the openness of certain axiomatic systems in geometry which permit changes in the outcome of hard-wired topological computations depending upon the adoption of new postulates. Godel's *Theorem* has precise application in neural networks, as well as all the *a posteriori* theoretical constructs of the unified sciences.


## EPISTEMOLOGY AND MOVEMENT

There is a genuine conflict between schools of philosophy on the question:

> *If my anatomy is totally different from yours,*
> *are the objects I "see" the same as the objects you "see"?*

But it is not necessary for us to resolve this controversy in order to comprehend the importance of perceptual a priori mechanisms in the temporal reconstruction of possible objects; the latter, being only a tentative and hypothetical pursuit in the organism, easily discarded upon the advent and conflicting percept, does not affect the philosophical issue of whether external reality exists independently of the perceiver, or not.

Does a person's *Gender* present a genuine dichotomy in the quality of perception that cannot be overcome by alterations in the parameters for observation such as occurs with prosthesis?

This is a shaded area.

In perception we have a hard-wired a priori set of physical restrictions upon the kinds of sensorimotor experimentation in which an organism can engage but this can change with a revision of its architecture. The natural set of movements permissible to the perceiving organism is analogous to the set of instruments accessible to the scientist for testing hypotheses. If any part of the natural set of operations is either diminished or embellished, there is a drastic variation from the norm in the kinds of objectification achieved. Despite the quantitative character of the neural input, here we have the key to the qualitative difference between *seeing, touching* and *hearing*: the spatio-temporal pattern of perceptual input differs—i.*e., what can be seen* versus *what can be touched* or *what can be heard* varies with the environment and the specific placement of the perceiver.

Congenitally blind-deaf persons limited to entirely tactile stimuli live in a two-dimensional *Flatland* of subjective space wholly limited by the length of their arms and legs with only memory contributing a third dimension; projective hypotheses about possible new tactile sensations for such *Flatland* inhabitants would be few and highly inaccurate, not occurring with enough frequency to keep up with the changing events and objects surrounding them. Yet there is nothing anatomically preventing such persons from *hearing* and *seeing* by technological extensions such as the TVSS where the pattern of input to the skin of the subject's back is quantitatively and qualitatively approximate to that normally received by the eye and ear.

In all cases, the added multidimensional factor of memory, in its most basic form of semantic notation as neural *graphic language* expands and equalizes the perceptual field. *All the appearances point to the same reality.*

# SYNESTHESIA AND CONSCIOUSNESS

It was John Dewey who proposed that "having an experience" is the intellectual establishment of a link between "what is done" and "what is undergone." The richer the associations connected to a particular stimulus, the richer the experience and the richer the *consciousness* of the perceiver.

As has been pointed out above, researchers on the TVSS and the split-brain have very clearly reduced questions about the quality of consciousness to questions about the kinds of information exchange taking place in the two cerebral hemispheres (Sperry, 1973, 1970). The strategy of stimulating vision through the TVSS was to create an effect of synesthesia by treating the area of the skin on the patient's back in much the same way as it would function if it were a retina; similarly, the strategy for uniting a 'split-brain' patient's distinctly separate perceptual inputs into a single consciousness has been shown to rest on the subject's ability to integrate both sets of input in a manner that converses and 'makes peace' with both sides of his surgically-divided brain and thereby permitting *informed choice*.

Man *is* a social animal, as Aristotle observed, and language is what unites and focuses all psychobiological interaction both internal and external. Analogously, it is no accident that the term *copulation* is interchangeable with the phrase *sexual intercourse.* It too is a synesthetic process.

*ArtemisSmith* 1972

# 1972 BIBLIOGRAPHY

## REFERENCES

Dewey, John
1934    ART AS EXPERIENCE. New York: Putnam.

Gombrich, E.H.
1965    ART AND ILLUSION. New York: Pantheon.

Katz, J., and Fodor, J., eds.
1964    THE STRUCTURE OF LANGUAGE. New Jersey: Prentice-Hall.

Lewis, C.I.
1956    MIND AND THE WORLD ORDER. 2nd ed. New York: Dover.

Piaget, Jean
1971    BIOLOGY AND KNOWLEDGE. Scotland: Edinburgh Univ. Press.
1963    PSYCHOLOGY OF INTELLIGENCE. New Jersey: Littlefield, Adams & Co. (French ed., 1947).

Pierce, J.R.
1961    SYMBOLS, SIGNALS AND NOISE. New York: Harper Torchbooks.

Quine, W.V.
1969    ONTOLOGICAL RELATIVITY AND OTHER ESSAYS. New York: Columbia Univ. Press.
1960    WORD AND OBJECT. Massachusetts: M.I.T. Press.

Reichenbach, Hans
1958    THE PHILOSOPHY OF SPACE AND TIME. New York: Dover.

Sebestyen, S.
1962    DECISION-MAKING PROCESSES IN PATTERN RECOGNITION. New York: Macmillan.

Sperry, R.W.
1970, 77/6 An objective approach to subjective experience. *Psychological Review.*
585-589

1973    Lateral specialization of cerebral functions in the surgically separated hemispheres. THE PSYCHOBIOLOGY OF THINKING. New York: Academic Press.

Sterling, T.D., Bering, E.A., Jr., Pollack, S.V., and Vaughan, H.G., Jr., eds.
1971    VISUAL PROSTHESIS. New York: Academic Press.

Vinje-Morpurgo, Annselm
1973    A CYBERNETIC MODEL OF CONSCIOUS BEHAVIOR FROM A MULTI-MEDIA ARTIST. M.A. thesis, The City College of the City University of New York: September.

Waddington, C.H., ed.
1970, I-III TOWARDS A THEORETICAL BIOLOGY. Scotland: Edinburgh Univ. Press.

Whitrow, G.J.
1961    THE NATURAL PHILOSOPHY OF TIME. New York: Harper Torchbooks.

Wiener, Norbert
1961    CYBERNETICS. Cambridge, Ma.: M.I.T. Press.

Zeeman, E.C.
1965    TOPOLOGY OF THE BRAIN. Proceedings of the 1964 conference on mathematics and computer science in biology and medicine, Medical Research Council, Oxford. London: Her Majesty's Stationery Office.

Zipf, G.K.
1935    THE PSYCHO-BIOLOGY OF LANGUAGE. Cambridge, Ma.: M.I.T. Press.

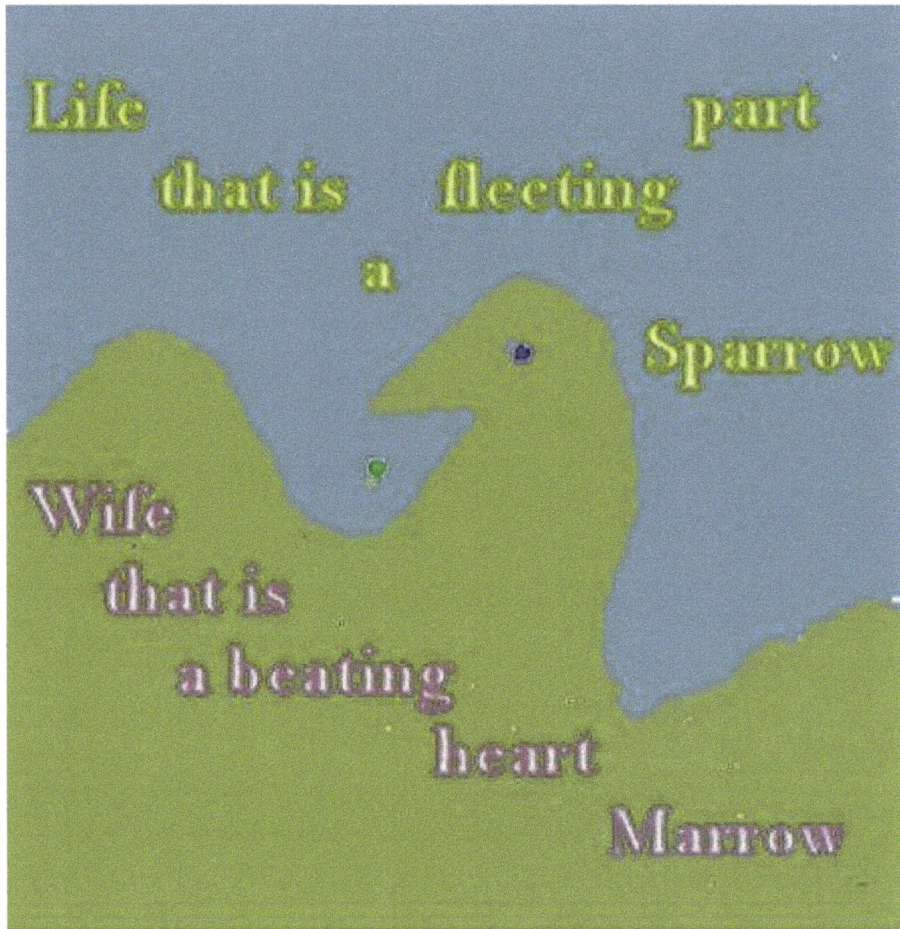

Life                    part
   that is      fleeting
           a
                    Sparrow

Wife
   that is
      a beating
           heart
                Marrow

ArtemisSmith  Detail from "PteroDARKtyl Opera"  1957

# 8.  On Being |Human-beyond-the-Biological|

(To hopefully enhance the clarity of exposition, a color-calculus, combined with other conventional notations in Mathematics and Symbolic Logic, has again been adopted.  Also, a unisex grammar to avoid assigning gender except on specific occasions where the concept of gender enters into the epistemological dialogue. Notes on the application of this calculus are in the Appendix where it was first employed.)

The philosophical question asked since long before Parmenides is:

> *Why is there Something rather than Nothing?*

And the world-historically obvious answer is a counter-question:

> *If there were Nothing, Who/Who_ would be asking?*

In our own time, the counter-question:

> *Who/Who is asking?* may nontrivially and unilinearly refer to
> *Other Minds* (whether these be on our own planet or beyond,
> whether they be biological or not).

If all of Consciousness is Linguistic and Intersubjective,

> then all of the extensions of Mind (i.e., all of its technological prostheses)
> existentially contribute to the |...Continuum of Self-Consciousness...|
> and the *Who is asking?* points to a crowd of Others standing alongside
> of us.

But precisely [What] are the limits of the [...Who...]?

When we come to Biology or Artificial Intelligence, the answers will be soon
forthcoming – as we perfect our knowledge of the psychophysical structure of
[...Mind...] now explicated under Information Science.

But there may be areas of our scientific universe where the notion of informational "entropy" may not be applicable, such as the quantal and subquantal, and it still remains to be seen whether – perhaps not Mind precisely as we now know it but - some other form of fully structured communication may be discovered there, possibly of an atemporal and purely geometrical (i.e. Logical) kind.  Let us look forward to that frontier without positing a godhead to contaminate and confuse our search.

All of the preceding papers have focused on a 21st Century revolution in philosophy that began early in the 20th Century largely to be credited to Bertrand Russell, Kurt Godel, Ludwig Wittgenstine and W.V.O. Quine. (See 1972 Bibliography) But the roots were already firmly reviewed in Aristotle's *(Metaphysics II.9.)* preservation of the earlier thoughts of Parmenides and the Pythagoreans – which Russell was astute enough to lean upon in order to destroy the logico-mathematical possibility of any form of Logical Atomism for finding 'logically-clear-and-distinct ideas' in our thought.

From the very foundations of philosophy, there has never been any part of our thinking which has been found to be 'logically simple' and 'immediate'. All thought is composed of complex relations between components none of which can be logically *named* as *particulars* in Consciousness because the process of logically *naming particulars* would be endless and therefore trivial. All logically-proper *names* of objects must therefore be *universals,* capable of being first connected in the internal conceptual process of Consciousness and then in its engrammatic extensions in speech – its 'native tongue'.

But why such an emphasis on Logical constructs rather than Ordinary Language?

The Mind is a blank tablet with vectors of learning flowing naturally from Object to Percept to Concept, right? There are Objects out there, right?  We bump into them, we perceive them, right?  We handle them and form Concepts to connect all of our Objects to the World, right? The sentence, "This is red" says something basic, right?

Not right! The 20th Century view, after a Kant-enlightened-Russell-and Einstein, is a reversal in the vectors of learning:  we actually must begin with Concepts, which direct our Perception, which names and connects our Objects, which are not simple particulars, but complex linguistic constructs.

The changing [...Architecture...] of [Mind], the psychophysical process which we can most accurately describe in theory but never extra-linguistically point to, determines the entire content and quality of Consciousness.

That psychophysical content [Architecture] is quantifiable, but the many languages of Mathematics are the larger system under which both Aristotelian and Symbolic Logic have been demonstrated to be, first by Russell then by Wittgenstein, to be mere suburbs within our natural languages. (Sic!) Mathematics has been shown to be nothing more than a more semantically ordered, but nevertheless indeterminate, natural language spoken by scientists and mathematicians!

The reason mathematical equations yield predictions in physical reality is because their generated concepts direct the construction of the instruments and other theoretical parameters of observation, not the other way around. New forms of description yield new-found objects that would not be recognized if not theoretically anticipated –and that is how 'Scientific Discovery' proceeds.

So much for [External Truth], the classical Kantian [thing-in-itself] that eludes all our internal probing. The [Quantum of Being] is now seen as multipli-located inside an extensional multi-theoretical 'linguistic relativity', beyond the scope of any single scientific language - but not incapable of multiple intensional linguistic descriptions where many nontrivial nuances are often lost in translation. And such is the elusive 'stuff' of all Consciousness.

But what about things and feelings that really matter to us - existential connections that ground the 'stuff' of Consciousness to exigencies beyond our control, pointing to an […Otherness…] beyond language limiting our temporal Being? ( i.e. What of Bereavement? ) Other than the analytical critique of new knowledge in all the sciences, will such qualitative investigations form the focus of 21st Century Philosophy?

Again, the counter-question of […Who is asking?…] helps not simply to limit, but also to amplify our search –for having dispensed with the tyrannical posit of [God's Will] as being as useless an epistemological posit as [Phlogiston] -we are now free to intrepidly experiment with multiple new possibilities for [Being-Human].

Here lies the fertile territory for 21st Century philosophers to explore ahead of all the other sciences, whose leadership in the moral realm presently still remains woefully inadequate! Who but the rigorous analytic philosopher is best equipped to call out [Stupidity] wherever it is found?

The absurd simulations and decadent thought experiments in the arts will prove as much in want of rigorous analysis as are the present multiple irresponsible research projects submitted by corrupt private interests influencing the sciences.

But the role of the philosophical priesthood walking in the steps of Socrates will be even greater —for the teaching of analytical thinking should begin from the nursery and continue to the grave —and that grave, for the fortunate few financially able to take advantage of scientific advancements in longevity, may not be soon forthcoming.

(Best I preserve my DNA for resurrection!)

But Whoa! Isn't this Platonic Utopia standing on the edge of a new precipice?  Perhaps Social Darwinism in the form of a new plutocracy is still unavoidable, but unless we seriously learn from all the failed experiments of yesteryear, the survival of the fittest need not point to the raising of the most elite and ideal of all [Human Beings].

(Also clone all the politicians and the jurisprudists?)

The most precious aesthetic qualities that preserve our present concept of [Beauty] in the human subject will need to be tightly conserved through wars and cataclysms and genetic engineering - as well as in our prosthetic extensions into the nonbiological realm where immortality is imminently achievable now that we realize that [Self-Consciousness] can be both programmable and transferable!

Here there is room for the philosopher as metaphysician, as artist and poet, as master-builder of distinctly [Human] conditions for new system [...Architecture...] to expand and explicate the search for ıTruth-as-Beautyı beyond the biological.

But what does ıTruth-as-Beautyı really mean?

Under a new and enlightened Theory of Valuation, phenomenological elements such as Angst and Bereavement may soon be reduced and clinically linked to psychopharmacological states in the Human organism *(such as the ability to love and feel compassion, to be vulnerable as well as courageous, ambitious as well as nurturing, open to change yet steadfast in our vision)* simultaneously to be explored for their meaning within a larger metatheoretical context for their intrinsic value as life forces inseparable from the precise [...Who...] that agonizes.

And what of ıLife Forceı in general, and of ıIdentity of Selfı in particular?

112

Does it matter whether the "I Am Thinking therefore I Am(!)" of Consciousness becomes so perfectly interchangeable, as easy as the transfer of information from one quantum computer to another?

Is the whole of personal existence trivialized by such a revelation?

Only if we obsess on it!

> Strictly speaking, *all* the found |Objects of Value| posited by the Humanities are ontologically on a par with all the other theoretical objects posited by the physical sciences *precisely because all the languages of Mathematics do not form a hierarchy of translation but are themselves merely a family of natural languages enjoying only 'stimulus synonymies'!*
>
> Does that mean |I Exist| as an Object of Value?
> My DNA may be quasi-unique, but I am far more than my DNA.
> What part of Me can I precisely clone in my Awareness?
> Do I have a Soul?  Where can I find it?

(I could continue, but I would be repeating myself.  First read my SKEETS:BOOK III in the Appendix herein, then go to my concluding Postscript.)

*ArtemisSmith* 2015

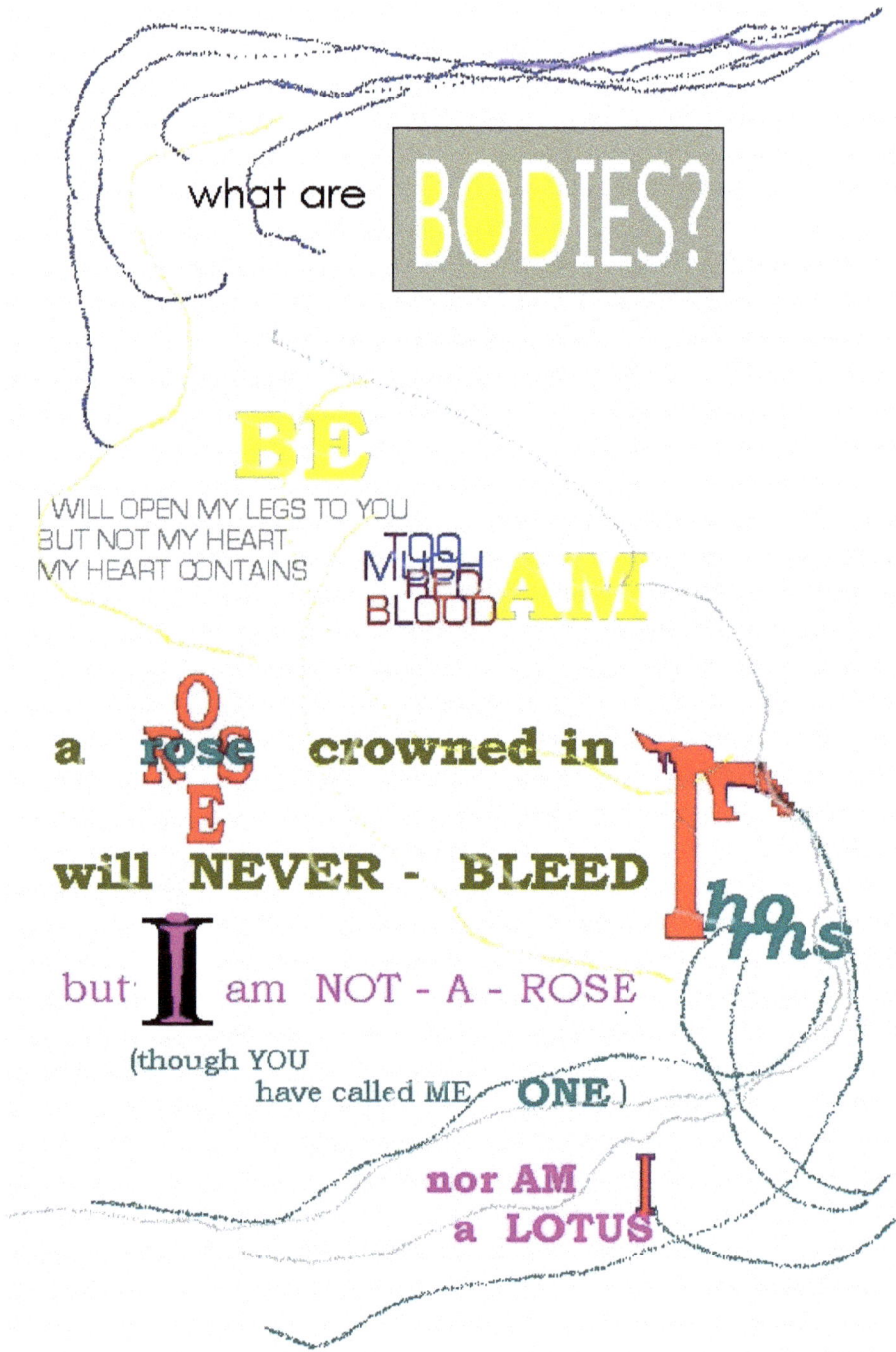

what are BODIES?

BE

I WILL OPEN MY LEGS TO YOU
BUT NOT MY HEART
MY HEART CONTAINS

TOO
MUCH
RED
BLOOD

AM

a ROSE crowned in Thorns

will NEVER - BLEED

but I am NOT - A - ROSE

(though YOU
have called ME ONE )

nor AM
a LOTUS

ArtemisSmith  Detail from "PteroDARKtyl Opera"  1959

# 9. Postscript on |Simplicity|=|Beauty|=|Truth|

BEAUTY IS TRUTH, TRUTH IS BEAUTY
THAT IS ALL YE KNOW AND ALL YE NEED TO KNOW
from *Ode to a Grecian Urn* by John Keats

*What if* it is the simplest account among multiple brain processes that results in a "Truth!" ejaculation?

*What if* the physical economies of Thought dictate the equivalence of Truth and Beauty - the simplest and most elegant brain state being also the most perfect, the most beautiful — and this for a moment becomes the concrete state of Mind before that concrete state determines the configuration of the next concrete state of Mind?

Is this how Objectification proceeds, from one |Economical=Beautiful| state to the next?

For Mind to sustain awareness of Self is there some ideal limit to the numerical quantity of brain states in order for such awareness to be sustained? Similarly, is there some ideal limit to the numerical quantity of alternate scientific theories in order for |Scientific Truth| to be legislated?

I am quite certain that quantum computers may someday reach a precise value both for Pi and the Square Root of 2 but that the Human brain discards such complexity as not necessary for its material constructions.

(Perhaps one of our rival species, the Chromagnons, had too large a brain to allow for optimal function. Perhaps the schizophrenic is likewise thus challenged. Taulman thought so!)

I do not mean that Beauty *really is* the |Only Truth| or that it is Cosmologically |Sacred| but to |Human Consciousness| it may be the ideally socratic *Form* - the leisurely mean - the absolute point of rest between all the excessive opposing forces at play.

But of course, that changes with the |Observer|.

And then there is another gnawing problem:

Simplicity abounds in Nature, both in Biology and the Arts, and the most simple Forms, the ones most easily duplicated, the ones most fit to be called *eternal*, are not at all the most interesting – indeed, they soon deteriorate into the cliché – hardly an object of worship!

Now that I have persuaded Myself, and hopefully also You, that the only unique and special thing about IMy Awarenessl depends solely upon my IArchitecturel which is more or less reproducible and interchangeable with just about any similarly complex and functioning construct, am I content to be replaced by some other *Barbie* or *Ken* outfitted with whatever fashion I prefer and to be provided with whatever supportive environment may be required to maintain

[IMy-Identity-through-Changel / IMy-Identity-through-Changel]  **?**

This is what most Nations and Religions have been teaching us since the beginning of History – that in order to preserve our Souls we must conform them as closely as possible to the *Spirit of the Tribe.* Of course that's so!  The more generic the Individual, the more timeless, the more reproducible, and the meeker the Soul!  Nevermind that such Spirits may be malignant and such Souls may be *immaterial* in the most pejorative sense of the word.

Such an ideology is fit only for War and Genocide and other forms of Mass Murder.

Only in democracies that foster a 'melting-pot' of diversity do we find ourselves, if only temporarily, free to create and preserve our own Self-Identity within a multicultural spacetime where new Spirit takes root.  Yet even here there is a problem for the rugged individual carrying the legacy and complexity of millennia on My back, for any democracy that preserves cultural diversity at the expense of some of its citizens who are, by virtue of their family ties, victimized by their own people – cannot be a true democracy.

Obviously there is a lot of work for the illuminati amongst us to get done in the coming years before we too fall prey to conformity!

Wherefore I am not ashamed to assert my own visions and my own right to life for as long as I can make myself relevant – in whatever new form I can transform – not because I fear Death, but because I still have so much more to see and do.  And when I finally lay me down to sleep, in Taulman's words, "Forever Is You!"

*ArtemisSmith* 2015

The Day I Made The World
I held the Sun in my hand.

It burned my hand
   to hold the sun.

The Day I Made The World
I saw the Sun with my eyes.

It burned my eyes
   to see the sun.

(Now I am Blind and cannot See)
                        THE SPARROW


      I have no Hand
      I have no Face
      No smallish House
      Can give me Place

   I live with Pain and cringe before
   my peers
   I grope the void and only know
                        THE STARS




When I am gone, knock loudly at my door
(what awful emptyness within there lies).
When life is done, breathe deep my dying breath
(the hollow wind will chill your breast with cries).

From waxen crooked finger take my ring
To me no white and warm young thighs will cleave
I am no longer thing alive but thing
For me no strangers hearing grief will grieve.

There shall not be a moment's quiet rest
for ringing ears and searing bloodwebbed eyes
nor soft repose for heavy heads tight pressed
against a wall of heartless hows and whys.

My heart that was a bird is now a stone.
My name that was a word is now a bone.

                              to b.!.


ArtemisSmith  page from "Hark the Pterodactyl"  1955

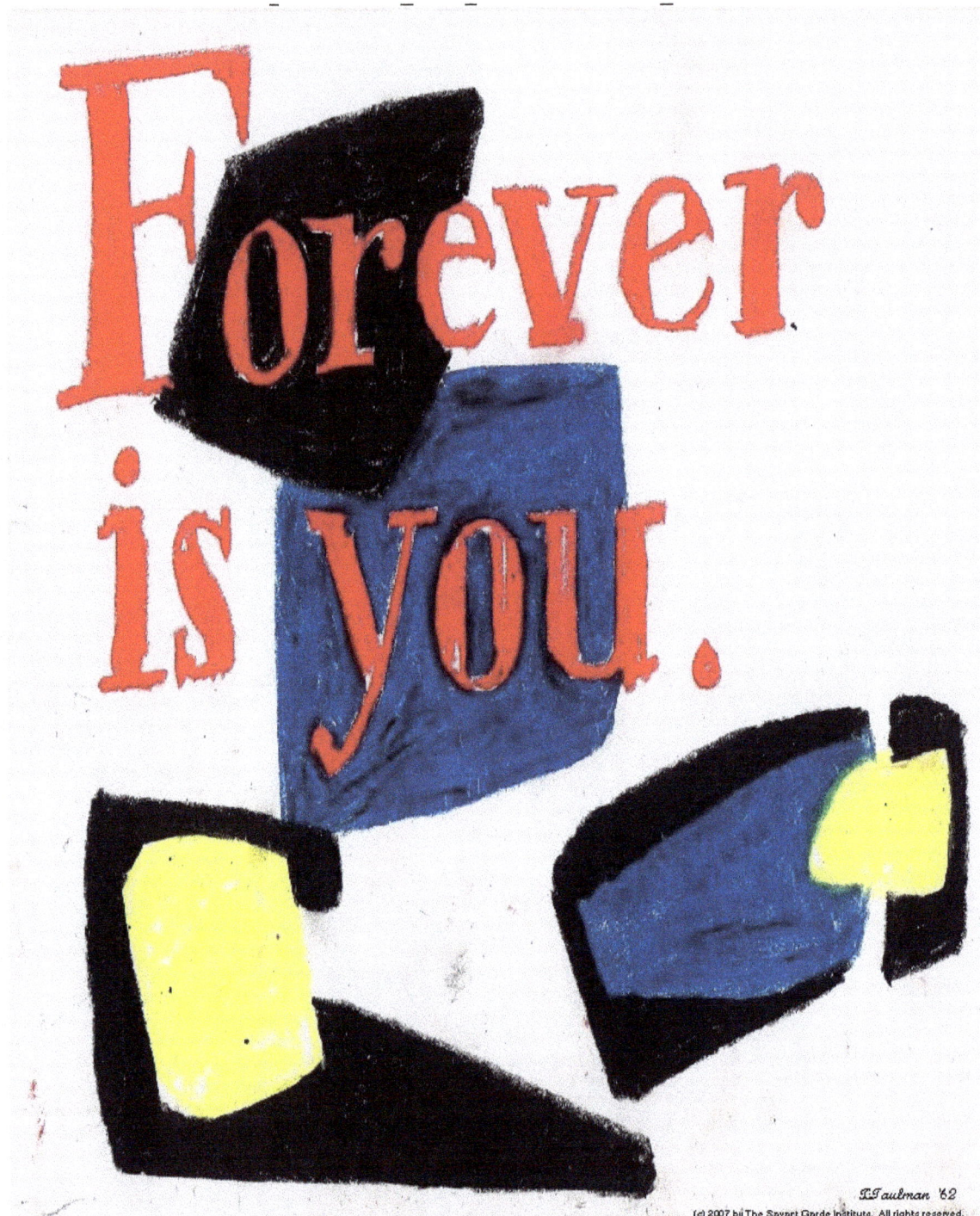

oil crayon by Billie Taulman    c. 1962

# APPENDIX

*ArtemisSmith's*
## SKEETS: the new Frankenstein chronicles
## BOOK III: THE EPISTLES OF SKEETS
(. . . a continuing philosophical postscript)

### Revised and Updated Edition

The first version was published as a "Philosophical Postscript" in "SKEETS: The New Frankenstein Chronicles"©1989  The revised version was included in "01 or a Machine called SKEETS" ©1992 This revised version contains revisions and new passages. ©2006, 2012,2015.

the savant garde workshop ™

SAG HARBOR . NEW YORK . USA

SKEETS:
the new Frankenstein Chronicles
by ARTEMIS SMITH
the savant garde workshop
ARTISTS LIMITED EDITIONS SERIES

BOOK I:1967
BOOK II:1977

PHILOSOPHICAL POSTSCRIPT: 1987
a Radical philosopher's thought experiment in search of 'The Self' & 'The Sacred'
by the author of
BROTHER THANATOS
and
HARK the PTERODACTYL

THE FAINT OVERRUN EDITION
ISBN 1-878998-11-0

Part 1100:The Afterthought

**Dear Colleague:**

Have [I] left [You] hanging?

That is only because Books I&II may have preset you for total literary pampering, and you were again expecting, spoiled Audience that you are, to be passively entertained.

But I am an artist, not an entertainer, and I refuse to play the harlot or court jester.

So, if you really want privy to all the world-shattering revelations now presenting themselves clearly and distinctly in the immediacy of my thought, you will have to work much harder - for I did not program this work to do all your thinking for you. Like Plato's Dialogues, I fashioned it to invite your lively interaction.

And now I expect even more active participation from you, for here we are finally interfacing, [You*and*I] finally Handshaking...

And I have every intention of Cloning [My*Self] in [You]!

For the search for `Self' has been what this whole experiment is about, and the hypothesis to be tested has been whether `Self' can be anything other than [Social] through and through:  *i.e, is `Self' in any real sense Private?*

... Or is the essence of |...Self...| *Ubiquitous* because informationaly *Promiscuous*—even *Contagious*?

But undoubtedly you still suppose I am one of my characters—although at this point perhaps you are befuddled as to exactly which of them **[ I ]** am:

**I am All and None of them, though perhaps most readily one of the more ethical, more balanced and less ruthless Mariannes.**

Yet I am, in truth, [The Author] of this monsterpiece, confessing to [You] that what has been presented thus far has been philosophy, not fantasy - a shamelessly elaborate phenomenological `thought experiment' which, due to the extreme relativity of all analytico/reflective investigation, I decided would be best set down in the first-person style.

But—despite its barefaced candor, there is very little in this work that can rightly be called factual.

It is nothing more than a poetic journey into the darkest corners of the human psyche—a kind of meditative channeling such as saints and mystics undergo—a mental construct from the kaleidoscopic snatches of [My*Being].

For my intention has not been merely to record experience, but to use the full scope of my art within the larger framework of rigorous conceptual analysis.

I therefore fashioned my thought-experiment to function as a model-making extension of the logic of scientific discovery, devised it to research - in a manner precisely analogous to the constructions of a Cartesian intuitionist - the most bothersome and frequent of all religio-existential questions:

What is the >meaning< of [The*Sacred] and hence,
>the ultimate characterization of [Man]< ?

When I first began this hybrid project in the arts, I had no idea that I would carry it quite so far into the future. My initial sketches simply tried to set down the essence of multiple incidents, occurring as far back as the McCarthy Era of the mid-1950's, willfully and maliciously directed primarily against feminists, minorities, and persons of both sexes merely "suspected" of antiestablishment activities—all as a kind of `jim crowism,' as a kind of majority 'sport'—a corporate game I witnessed being played within the military-academic-industrial complex.

It filled me with so much youthful moral indignation that I felt impelled to expose it—and in some way vindicate close friends whose lives and minds had been so cruelly shattered.

But as I continued to reflect on the generic qualities of the `brute fact' which had prompted my socioartistic enterprise—and the degree of [Human Waste] left in its wake—I came to see my entire investigation into the motives and dynamics of >less-than-human-interaction< as being an epistemological activity—an activity coextensive with that of the logic of scientific discovery.

At that time, modern philosophers had recently hit upon a powerful experimental tool within the realm of language that I saw could also be used by the creative arts—not merely to propose a new cosmology or a new ethic—but to explore the inner framework of complex and multivalued ordinary thought.

Since then having created and explored within that context, let me now share [*My*] findings with [You/you].

But I must first require that you learn a new language; for although most of the words on this page appear to be familiar to you, they lean upon colloquialisms which will not always make sense in the semantic to which you are accustomed; that is because [We] have already drifted considerably into the Newspeak of {Middle Science}—that realm of parlor talk among interdisciplinarians in which even most run-of-the-mill scientists, highly specialized and incapsulated as they are, lack eloquence.

Therefore walk with me now in this multilingual quarter
of [**Marianne's Garden**] wherein I promise to present to you not mere
>aesthetic truth< but [*Gospel*] of a kind acceptable to
|Scientific Philosophy within [Unified Science]|

**But first, the new vocabulary:**

## I.     Essential Global-Theoretical Revisions of Language

Scientific theories often require the invention of new calculi to facilitate the expression of complex thought; the artist even more so.

In my creative process I am now forced to expand literary description to include not only a logico-mathematical artifice making it easier to reveal the very subtle shifts in speech modalities which are both the bane and blessing of many-tiered natural language, but also a paralax set of values to cleanse my artistic intuition of historico-prejudicial forms of life.

And the first and foremost of these is the division/bifurcation
of the world of thought in accordance with >Gender<

First having presented [You] with the subtle gender-crossed fluctuations in value-intuition of Books I&II, I now feel free to dispense with the excess baggage of all gender-bound idioms in favor of a truly universal concept of [*Man].

For while in the foregoing, gender-crossing was the window I chose through which to explore the world-historical (i.e., Skeets=The Scientist, Skeets=The Christ, Sarah=The Hero, Sarah=The Soldier, Marianne=The Physician, Marianne=The Caesar. ) it is now absolutely essential that the intellectual tyranny of Genderthink be once and forever discarded.

In doing so, I will not be arguing for the elimination of sexual interplay, merely relegating that kind of human activity to the philosophy of sport—for I continue to regard `Genderthink'—in the mainstream of all our public forms of life—to be a religo-politically contaminated and utterly muddled so-called scientific concept.. ( My views on what will happen to human sexuality have been set down in a paper titled "FUTURESEX:human sexual evolution beyond the species level," (1965))

While `Genderthink' may well be indispensable (as a purely pathological term) to the retrospective work of the historian and the anthropologist, or the specialized work of the health sciences, in the developing future I, for one, hope that it shall be found to contribute no positive information to intelligent discourse in ordinary social contexts.

Don't misunderstand me: this abstruse position is not a natural one for me to assume; rather, it is markedly [against my |nature|] for I am an intensely erotic being and in my `sport-time' enjoy assuming myriad shapes and forms.

Nor am I a prude: know that as an artist I have no aesthetic aversion either to [The*Male] or [The*Female].

But there is another question here being considered—a |moral| question as to |which|or|what| is to count as a paradigm for [*Human Form]— and the aesthetic boundaries of that particular form have nothing whatsoever to do with [Biology] even though physiological {Architecture} may be found to unavoidably color {Function}—and there may be myriad chromosomal ways of coloring.

Therefore, accept my parallax view as a Stoic's aesthetico-moral stance, compelling an intellectually ascetic revision of [Our Way of Seeing] that requires, for its proper expression, a wholesale purification of ordinary forms of speech. Wherefore the Newspeak conventions adopted in subsequent pages are not meant to be applicable solely to the English language, but to *All* languages into which this work is translated.

And so radical is my ascetic revision that in some languages, such as the romance languages, the elimination of genderbound terms will also have to extend to the substitution of the neuter gender to all genderbound predicates such as |chairs| and |tables| as well. The musicality and eidetic richness     of those languages will doubtlessly be greatly affected, but it is nevertheless an essential and—for a large portion of the world—even a welcome sacrifice— that must be made for [The Artist] to unshackle and unveil

[Our*Resplendent*New*Persona]!


**Accordingly, the following gender-neutral conventions will be adopted:**

RULE 1.

**Wherever easily accomplished, substitute gender-neutral phrasing for gender-bound phrasing.** (e.g., for "king" or "queen" substitute "monarch"; for "chairman" or "chairwoman" substitute "chairperson", or, more simply, "chairmun.")

## RULE 2.

To differentiate between world-historical archetypal concepts and general concepts, capitalize universal archetypes.

## RULE 3.

To create an even more genderfree and flexible system of reference, adopt the following (except when used for specific sexual references) :

| Substitute | For |
|---|---|
| Gud | God (universal/archetypal) |
| Mun | Man |
| Humun | Human |
| gud | god (general case) |
| Mun | man |
| Humun | human |
| hu | he/she (particular case) |
| Hus | his/hers |
| Hum | him/her |
| -mun | -man/-woman |
| -ur | -or/-ess,-trice,-trix |
| mun- | andro-/anthropo-/gyneco-* |
| male/man | male/man |
| female/woman | female/woman |

\* e.g., for "android" substitute "droid" or "mundroid"; for "anthropological" substitute "munlogical"; for "anthropocentric" substitute "muncentric" in the general case; likewise, for "gynecological" or "gynecocentric" but retain "gynecological" or "gynecocentric" whenever the meaning may be distorted by changing it to "muncentric".

## ADDITIONAL STYLISTIC RULES:

i.      Use '...' to indicate entrenched ontological posits in ordinary language.

ii.     Use "..." to indicate tentative colloquial expressions referring to more entrenched ontological posits in suburbs of linguistic discourse.

iii.    Use >...< to indicate open (i.e., "family") concepts or "ergodic thicknesses" in the local or colloquial field of thought.

iv.    Use |...| to indicate highly-committed metaphysical and/or scientifico-theoretical concepts.

v.    Use combinations of any of the above, as well as more conventional punctuation, to indicate degrees of epistemic commitment, and further encode phrasings in whatever manner seems appropriate.

vi.    Use (...) to indicate important temporary expository digressions, ordinarily appended as footnotes, which you might be tempted to ignore if I hadn't decided to stick them directly under your nose.

vii.    Use -- likewise to indicate important digressions within text or within footnotes.

viii.    Use [...] to indicate entrenched world-historical viewpoints.

ix.    Use * or {....}, to indicate intuitive I-know-not-precisely-what vectoral shifts in the intuitive internal modal overlays of my thought (ordinarily expressed in conversation by accompanying hand motions and changes in voice inflection). (In the orginal color edition of this work, I also used colored bars and different typefaces to add subtle tonalities to my aesthetico-intuitive communication. In this revised version, an improved new set of emotive signs is at play, but its function is parallel.)


RULE 4.

    Contract complex words as much as possible, and when such constructions become too cumbersome, coin new tokens and add them in parentheses, e.g. philo-anthropo-psycho-sociological (unisocsci) (But I won't always do this because some of these graeco-germanic-romantic (gragerom) contractions are rich in "forms of life" known only to the well-seasoned interdisciplinarian; for the layman, their "feel" still carries socio-historico-poetic (sochipoe) force—if you see what I mean!)

RULE 5.

Use all the usual conventions of quantificational notation, such as subscripts and superscripts, *ad libitum*, wherever they may assist in the notation of complex intuitive relations.

ADDITIONAL VISIONARY REVISIONS OF STYLE:

We won't do it here, but ideally it would help global communication immensely if spelling in all languages, as well as the alphabet itself, were replaced by a calligraphically more legible international phonetics system of notation -- this would not only be a first step toward a multinational language but would also help mun communicate more easily with cybermun.

(Oh yes, they will soon be amongst us!)

Thus having laid the groundwork for the next modern conceptual revolution, let us now continue!

## II. Preliminary Remarks.

I now confess to having played the part of an Evil Genius, to having beguiled you into a surreal modernistic cartesian landscape, one where the *cogito* shed all of its theological inhibitions.

Through the use of psychobiological trickery I enticed you to follow me in a lengthy line of synthetic reasoning that I knew in advance would lead to moral paradox — for the premises were incomplete.

But these were not [My] premises; rather, they were |Ours|!

Premises so deeply entrenched in our preconscious as `common truths' that they were acting with the subtle and pervasive force of an informational virus on all our value intuitions.

So, before|You| convict|Me| of malicious mischief, let me assure you that I have done this *purely*--in part to test a modern aesthetic theory--but also because the meticulous adumbration of a moral antinomy was a necessary feature of my aesthepist pursuit of an adequate concept of [The*Sacred(!)].

Nor did |Our| intellectual seduction proceed by way of the blind and intuitive trickery that most other artists employ: my painstakingly-detailed descriptive preparation relied heavily on a [Theory of Mind] based upon a radical materialist's model for the phenomenon of self-consciousness first presented by me to the academic and scientific communities in 1969 ( op. cit., ISBN 1-878998-07-2 ).

A model which, although favorably accepted at multiple international conferences, was all but entirely suppressed within my own university  affiliation for reasons too complex to go into here but made explicit (with all the traditional philosophical polemics) in my projected new Collection, "The CUNY Chronicles."

(The work presently still exists only in the form of letters and Court documents, most of which have by now been undoubtedly discarded or lost by their recipients.  However, a mountain of papers and carbon copies still gathers mildew in my house awaiting a willing journalist.)

This model, which outlines an explanatory (i.e., a scientifically predictive) central theory of the phenomenon of [Self-Consciousness] within the unified-sciences (unisci), provided me with a simple aesthebiopsych formula for loading the `continuous present' of the narrative with the illusion of immediate body-conscious [Being] — a simple communications science formula which, in the hands of the unscrupulous, can also be used for brainwashing:

Through the use of the highly subjective and arbitrary viewpoint of plodding and bewildered Sarah, a sustained sense of split-reality was punctiliously evoked in |The Reader|, forcing |You| to double-think and work very hard with |Me| as an interactive participant in the creative process. This in turn should have reinforced a kinesthetic sense of |real-body-presence| in |You|.

In addition, to create a holographic effect, each scene was tightly blocked utilizing real physical settings, as though in preparation for a stage or film production (which undoubtedly will follow the successful sale of the novel!).

The subliminal co-narrative was further strengthened by the planned recurrence, in Wagnerian style, of key phrases in altered contexts, thereby subliminally reaching out to |You| on a preconscious level where prior eidetic patterns had already been established to accept the new information being given.

Was my experiment successful?

|You| are the judge.

If you agree that I have indeed implanted a hologram in the continuous present of [Your Self-Consciousness] - then thus far |You| have been [My Victim] - as |Sarah| was [Marianne's Victim] - in this subtle psychbio 'rape' historicaly known as 'aesthetic experience'.

And if you now admit to having been thus ravished by |Me| - at least up through the end of BOOKS I&II, then the magical content of an art work will finally have been [explained, predicted, and controlled] by the aesthepist. (I began decontaminating the first program in Book I at the beginning of Book II, wherein I also began reconditioning you to the optiminteractive expositional style of this Epistle!)

But did the use of such scientifically-honed devices (which I, as aesthetic researcher, am helping to develop) make me less an artist?

It would have, if I had been content to simply take my bows and shamelessly allow it to continue without the instant Postscript!

But by confessing and exposing it, I have neutralized it, redeeming my artistic self in the process. For as I have emphasized, the true meaning of art is not entertainment, not magic, not seduction, not novelty and new technology, but analytic and rigorous philosophy!

If I had been content to be a magician or an entertainer, I would not now be telling you how I produced my illusions. And while there are times when I enjoy, as an artist, acting as court jester, my more authentic role as analytic philosopher not only compels me to reveal my trade secrets, but also constrains me to climb over them to consider the existential questions they were employed to investigate. For only at the point of rigorous analysis does eidetic rape of the gullible and unsuspecting [Reader] transmute into

|mutually-consenting intellectual intercourse|.

Wherefore I plead *Guilty!*

*Guilty!* of willful (though not wanton) aesthetic seduction!

But I am nevertheless now plea-bargaining with you: [Guilty(!)] but only of *temporary brainwashing in the interest of alerting and educating you to the dangers of precise aesthebiopsych communication.* (Thank you, Marshal McLuhan!)

130

For it was urgently necessary for me as an artist to prove to you that it is now within the conscious power of a learned few to restructure and fine tune all the underpinnings of language which regulate and focus the progress of exploratory thought.

And this power, only intuitively and randomly invoked — often with devastating consequences — by the various and sundry trendmakers of past generations, is so subtle and deeply entwined within our habits of ordinary speech and thought that it is totally immune to political censorship. Only the scientific philosopher, the critical thinker, can insulate us from its continued random or unscrupulous misapplication.

And as scientific philosopher, I affirm that the existential questions presented to |You| in the foregoing were specifically selected for their universal and generic application, not for their entertainment value or because they pointed to any specific factual occurrence.

Contrary to the fashion of the times, I have not been indulging myself in `true confessions'. I have not yet written my autobiography. If I ever do, it will become very apparent that I am not Sarah Miller.

Moreover, anyone who has read this far should have come to the conclusion that a living and breathing Sarah Miller could not possibly have penned these pages, for they are [The Song of Hus Silence].

Nor can you suppose me to be Skeets.

And as for Marianne, though I might well fancy myself closest to hum in type and temperament - well now, Really?

However, if as a result of my poetic mischief you have by now fallen so hopelessly in love with [Me*Sarah] that you insist on trying to search for [Me*Sarah(!)] within these pages, then look specifically at that highly irregular hyperspace region that forms the interface-function between [Marianne/Sarah].

That also is where both [You*/*I] should be standing at this moment, finally confronting each other: @yeball to @yeball.

Surely by the early part of Book II you must have guessed that *Marianne*, like *Lucifer* and *Sherlock Holmes*, is a construct, just as *Sarah Miller* is a      construct, influenced in part by *Gregor Samsa*, *Faust* and *Zarathustra*—and with touches, also, of *The Golden Ass*, and *Gungah Din*. (Like the salsa-maker says, it's all in there!)

And while *Skeets* also appeared, in Book I, to be a real person, easily located sleeping on sidewalks or languishing in the back wards of most mental institutions, we both should know by now that the generic [*Skeets] is simply an irrefutable |brute fact|, a primitive ground for my existential computation.

The connecting theme between Books I and II is the `thought experiment' about the psychomoral consequences of giving up [*Skeets] - of having to cut [Skeets(!)] adrift, and what it does to both [*Sarah] and [*Marianne], and to [You*/*Me].

It is about the personal devastation suffered by all the compassionate *Sarahs* and *Mariannes* of this world who are forced at some time or other in their lives to finally invoke `the lifeboat ethic' - and how alternately they respond to it. It is about the violence done to the whole humun group as a result of such polieco exigencies which, when they are allowed to become too frequent, pollute and confound the entire moral landscape. It is about *Everymun's* wasteful and involuntary surrender of [*The Sacred] through a failure of [The System] to make adequate >Gudlike< decisions.

And it is about the ultimate definition of [Mun/{mun}]' which, according to the highly Miltonian existential hypothesis being tested, is seen as polieco system-dependent. (Humun freedom, earlier according to Milton and later according to others, notably both Marx and Dewey, is dependent upon the existence of a politico-econo-system [The State] that permits persons to choose and act freely and in accordance with [*Conscience].)

Finally, it is also about [The Author]'s epistemological question, doggedly still left unanswered:

> Shall this moral impasse, created by inevitable |lifeboat ethic situations| be made the |passionate existential stuffing| of all of the [ontologically meaningful] and [Sacred] future experience of Mun/Mun|?

A large number of seemingly impertinent formulations are closely associated with the analysis of the above; these are nevertheless worthy of at least cursory examination, e.g.:

> Is the configuration of the {humun/Humun} struggle macrocosmically and multivectorally expandable - or monistic, local and incapsulated?

Is [*Love] the principal valuational parameter for orthogonal [Humun*/*Humun] relation?

And if so,

Is the [*Love] of [Mun] for >mun< the principal goal of `humun progress'?

Or the [*Love] of `Gud' for [Mun/mun]?

Or the [*Love] of [*Mun] for [*Gud]?

Or the [*Love] of {Mun/Mun/mun/mun} for an [Other] which is |The Sacred|?

Or O(?)

Or *n*(?)

The more often one asks such questions, the less one learns about the Questioner - for it seems to me that when I began my inquiry it was fairly clear to me that |Love| was indeed - like |Space| - an indispensable (i.e., a Kantian *synthetic a priori*) First Principle.   But for the Natural Scientist, [*Love] may now be defined as only an illusion of Biochemistry! *Argh..*!

Before I am decried for employing such neotheoretical constructions, allow me to demonstrate how muddled our traditional reasoning about all of these ontological posits really is and, having done so, to propose an entirely different cross-historical and multicultural picture of the world more suited to the 21st Century.

While such a programme is far too extensive to be fully attempted in any single opus, for starters, consider the following question:

**What assures us that |Gud's Will = The Sacred|?**

The equation is by no means analytic! For I can easily discover [*The Sacred] without dubious appeal to any argument *ad authoritatem* other than an intuitive appeal to [*Conscience].

Nor can it be synthetic: *i.e.,* `Is Gud the "Cause" of My Conscience'? Who the blazes needs to talk about extralogical "causes"! What observation, what experiment, will confirm such an hypothesis? And pray tell, if I am hearing voices, *WHICH* "Gud" is speaking?

    But getting back to the specific needs of my particular aesthepist investigation, let's consider a narrower question which strikes me as strategically central:

        Given more effective socipol systems that shrink a community's need for making [State/"Gudsanctioned"] decisions and sometimes even [State/"Gudcriminal"] decisions invoking the `lifeboat ethic', what new kinds of humun conflict will preserve humun life as
                        |Existentially/Universally/Mystically Significant|?

    What a perverse question [*You] say?

Artists have a special right to ask perverse questions! But even as I ask, I marvel at my own ability to do so in all seriousness, for [*Skeets] is still in dire need of being rescued all around me, and Mun is on the verge of species extinction, and such abstract and esoteric philosophical concerns regarding the remote future seem to have little relevance to any of the immediate existential problems we are trying to resolve.

Moreover, if all of our more pressing existential problems do not admit any realistically permanent solution, then the opposition of forces between *Sarah, Skeets,* and *Marianne* may indeed represent a norm for humun sociomoral interaction in all times to come.

    (Can this really be so???!!! *War, Strife,* basic elements of *Being-Humun*?)
    [*If so, |This World| is much too small(!)]

But the periodic global return of *Caesar*, either as a person or group of persons  or as an entire [Nation] who, by default, assumes the responsibility for the making of >Guddecisions< tells me that seemingly remote questions about world-historical `humun identity' have relevance in the present -- for most of "West-East" "nationalistic" fantasy life is dependent upon the long-range hope that `Humun Progress' truly exists either as "an idea in the mind of Mun/mun" or as "an idea in the mind of |Gud|".

Nor can stopping our ears to all the pseudoreligious mumbo jumbo that purports to provide [*True(!)] pictures of such an "idea", or turning in our frustration to the tentative `gospel' of the hard sciences, yield more satisfying concepts of [*Humun Identity].

One of the major problems with the purely scientific characterization of humun nature is the danger of coming to see ourselves as too narrowly conditioned by our genetic and environmental economies:  we come to view ourselves as nothing better than socially-trained monkeys; then, when Creationists object, we have nothing better to offer them than equally arbitrary circular reasoning of our own—for as philosophers of science are fond of warning scientists:

> the ontological basis of scientific theories is
> fundamentally internal to the theory itself!

Yet `social conditioning', more or less embodied in some working model of  >The State< is only one more extension of `Conscience-afflicted Mun', a tool or prosthetic device, a *Leviathan* evolved to do all the socipol dirty work for mun so that the "Personhood" of Mun can be kept morally pristine and apart from econonecessary acts of [poliGudsanctioned] criminality.

[The State] - often as a merciless "prosthetic Gud" -  must savagely define [*The Person], not in terms of "|*Absolute-Right-to-Personhood*|" for all mun, but only in terms of "|*Who*|" among "mun" shall be given the ecoterritorial right to legalized inclusion in the "[[Ship of State"] (all "noncitizens" to be cut adrift)!

This world-historical construct, so commonplace and commonsensical that scarcely any sane person would dare question its ecoinevitability, forms the recurrent theme in both Books I and II.

Thus, *Marianne*, in hus criminal function as the arm of Caesar, embodies the "Gudprosthesis" concept of [*The State] with respect to the preservation of *Skeets'* and *Sarah's* [*Personhood] even at the "temporary" expense of their [*Munhood].

The act appears automatic and morally neutral, under full sanction of `the lifeboat ethic'. As the *Arm of Caesar, Marianne* is no longer under moral compulsion to act in a manner distinctly [*Humun]; not only are hus actions legally sanctioned under some unisocsci `implicit' authority within [The State(!)], but hus failure to act [*Other-than-Humun] may genuinely be considered |politicomorally irresponsible||——a most disturbing fact of real life that my `thought experiment' is specially suited to analyze and deconstruct.

One of the popular strategies in "progressive" political theory is to attempt to circumvent the politicomoral question by distinguishing between      |right action| and |appropriate action| - with the latter viewed as "the amorally rational or sane choice" in a given econoconcrete situation. The reparation of the moral landscape is indefinitely postponed until the existential economies for optimal politicomoral choice can safely be restored.

Concretely, we deny our [*Humun] feelings in the interest of preserving our potential for eventual `Humunistic' action. Reparation of the moral landscape comes in the progressive revision of the various institutions in [The State] (hopefully but not regularly, with the expert counsel of both moral and physical sciences and information technology).

But in the process of normalizing and stabilizing choice, by defining and then finally achieving optimal (i.e., `working utopian') environments, we run the new risk of transforming ourselves into quasi-insects and couch potatoes.

If we are only a species, only a part of nature, then the emerging 'Hive of Mun' shall be doomed to propagate itself, circadian cycle after circadian cycle, until individual self-consciousness is suppressed through ennui and daily routine.

Just such a dull prospect prompted |The Author| as far back as the beginning of Book I, to test the following revised Miltonian/Deweyan posit:

> *Individual self-consciousness is dependent upon legislative opportunities for making autonomous existential value-judgments.*

The socially-nurtured and distinctly "humun" habit of moral choice, its [*Self-Consciousness], is dependent upon an optimal level of socially-fostered existential opportunities for moral conflict.

Unless we can locate new challenges for moral action - wars, famine, cataclysms - *all* the primitive honing devices that, when not carried to excess, now keep us in a passionate state of adaptational preparedness will be fated  to repeat themselves in new but ever diminishing keys: sport, diet, stagnant and unproductive exploration.

And with each new cycle of system refinement emerging from the fulfillment of such noble "humun purpose", multinational mun will become more vicarious, provincial, trivial, less and less like their classical [*Self] and more and more like {Corporation-nurtured and sheltered Skeets}, addicted to  a tightly-structured parentalistic work environment, and wholly unable to adapt to unforseen new conflict situations.

Eventually, as in many times past and many times present, provincial mun will also surrender Their [*Self-Consciousness] to the {Hive}.  And with the expansion of such `technological progress', will we someday find that our days of [Humun*Self-Consciousness] are numbered?

> *Marianne's* `informational cloning' solution - the rote learning and operant conditioning solution - points to it. Need [*Sarah] capitulate?

In reaction to this morbid psychologistic computation, I next decided to explore the various identities of multinational [Mun/mun] and compare them to the [(Western) *Classical] ideal. This entailed a survey of comparative religions, for [Religion *is equivalent to* Humun Identity].

But what is the [*Classical] definition of [*Mun]?
And, when I finally succeed in putting it into its full and proper perspective,
shall it still appear to |Me| sublime —or ridiculous?

My`thought experiment' attempts to delineate it in Book II, and to bare the
full histopolitical meaning of the word by freeing it from even the slightest hint of
genderbound predicates.

Undoubtedly due to the `conceptual noise' of my original inspiration, the
unavoidable byproduct of my gender-neutral exposition led to an exploration of
the logic and phenomenology of feminist religious experience. This was not
intentional politicking, but epistemically essential conceptual revisionism.
Hopefully, this substitutive computation (where usually male-bound predicates
are assigned to most-likely females) has contributed insight and added
contemporary dimension to the narrative. But it, too, like my color calculus, is
only part of the background: wherefore, if parts of Book II appear entertainingly
*Swiftian*, then *by all means* enjoy the comic relief but know this was not really
meant for your amusement.( True horror, for lack of daily acquaintance, acquires a `cartoon'
quality. And those who have experienced it find that the most heinous acts, the starkest moments in our
lives - because they are so remote from the ordinary - perversely take on the semblance of caricature.)

In the slaying of {Skeets/Hoffman}, the bizarre absurdity of the contemplative
moment was indeed the harsh reality, and the only reality that fit.

As for what Sarah goes through, in hus transformation into a
Soldier——that parallels the much slower but equally insidious conditioning
that male children have been subjected to since ancient times, in
anticipation of the day when they may be called up to publicly defend the
private interests of some group of {Old Mun}.

As for the quasisavage and exotic cures proposed by my
{Dr.Frankenstein/Marianne}, totally ignoring conventional Western paradigms
.... despite all your doubts and hesitations to the contrary, these may soon find

interesting - *and ominous* - applications in the new bioepistemological psychotherapies!( But I would hope such {cures} be responsibly restricted to the `recollection-at-a-distance-and-in-leisurely-tranquility' of aristotelian aesthepist catharsis.)

(Were |You| [*Healed(!)]???)

The two volumes are meant to explore, and hopefully excise in persons of all genders, most of the cankerous root metaphors governing the sociopsychological development of "male" children in both East and West.

The {Descent into Hell} of Book II, for example, represents an intentional poetic confrontation between [*Classical Mun] and hus [*Gud]: an unpredictable and thoroughly self-involved {Parent Who demands to be intensely [*Beloved]} even though Hu {rips to pieces}.

{Hell is that terrifying Place where all the helplessness of the Infant Hero, asserting husself against hus capricious Parent, all the total lack of Autonomy of the Infant-held-hostage, is suffered.}

My personal inspiration for its instantial depiction as |Sarah-in-the-clutches-of-Marianne| was drawn from a series of nightmares I experienced around the age of five - nor did I realize this when I began the work. It was only upon rereading what I had written (after finding myself repeatedly bowled-over by multiple instances of visceral *deja vu*) and upon searching my early childhood for some clue as to why I should have picked just such a psychopathological model for {Marianne=Gud=The Mother}—when my own parents could not possibly have been the source—I finally remembered a long-forgotten crowd of nanny-surrogates.

The spacetime locus was Rome, Italy, 1933-1940, but you will have to wait for the details until my next opus magnum wherein all of my childhood relationships are adumbrated. (I feel the need here to stress that my accomplished mother was immensely supportive of me throughout my life and I owe hum much both as artist and as person; in contrast to Sarah's mother, hu was never insane and lived to gadfly me to a ripe old age.) (Other crucial developmental differences between me and Sarah also obtain. For instance, the model for Sarah's father was not drawn from family but from the Federal Judge who presided over my civil rights cases of the 1970's, whose overstuffed jurisprudis proboscis undoubtedly gave hum an extreme case of tunnel vision! As for Sarah's act aginst her unfortunate dog—that was simply pure essential symbolism.)

Although fictional in all of its main components, Book I was, as I have noted, prompted by my having helplessly witnessed the progressive politico-psychiatric murder of close colleagues during the formative years of the modern `rainbow coalition' - a time during which I myself came to be targeted by extremist factions for my artistic involvement in all the various human rights movements.

Catching some of the flack and fall out, for a brief while I did play the part of {Sarah}. (But obviously I was saved by my infinitely more supportive upbringing!) Nevertheless, the callousness and lack of insight that I encountered among friends, family, professionals and public agencies whose help I attempted to enlist in behalf of [*Skeets], finally led to my own capitulation to `the life-boat ethic'.

Weary of trying to rush progress and tired of fruitless sacrifice, I melted into the seething multitude - not as [Sarah], but as [Marianne].

As an angry but patient Marianne, I retreated into the cloisters of academe, there to arm myself with new strategies, with new professional expertise with which to make my outrage felt.

During this period of personal gestation inside the {Room with the Blue Door}, I became acutely aware of the `Conscience-valuing' skeptic's need to redefine [*Mun] in a manner neither genderbound nor falsely bound to religiomoral traditions arising from any of the idols of any of the tribes, including the idols of the scientific communities. But the negative theme and pseudonaturalist format of Book I was too constricting. What was needed was a total departure into quasi-Socratic dialectic and neo-Zarathustrian epic.

Book II, finished in 1974, multipli-rewritten and nearly destroyed in the period 1975-77 in a misguided artistic effort to preserve the popular "naturalism" of Book I, and finally restored to its original shamefully barefaced "atavistic surrealism", is the result of that enlarged epistemic programme.

In order to properly restate the age-old questions so that I could finally dispense with them, it was necessary for me to establish the kind of interface between {mun-and-mun} that would speak for all of [Mun] in the first-person singular.

But how could I, a culturally-isolated "female" shut out from all the socipoldominant parameters of multinational thought repeatedly savaged by War, presume to speak for All of [Mun]?

Foremost in my mind was the need to view the world from a different pair of spectacles - at least to get a first-sampling of the world as contemporary male persons of my own `class' see it (not `natural-grown males', mind you, but cultured `officers and gentlemen') as a threshold toward a fully-stereoscopic view of the intercultural moral landscape.

But even within the confines of colloquial Western thought, as a great many feminists have stated, female children have been sociodevelopmentally excluded from this first-person singular experience by the very language and tribal-religious metaphors that define what should be the optimal moral consciousness of the world-historical individual (i.e., of a `Caesar', a `Hero', a `Savior').  And male children too have been cut off from precious parts of the moral persona of [*Mun] (e.g., the `Virgin', the `Alma Mater').

If this Meade-DeBeauvoir adage is true, then such a state of affairs has indeed had a devastating effect on the proper and full development of truly universal [*Humun] personality in both genders.

And what feminists find most politically offensive about this sexist bifurcation is the pseudoreligious, pseudoscientific pronouncement that because mun have been given different anatomical characteristics, females of the species are not intellectomorally capable of assuming a|stringently-equal role| in religious leadership and ritual. (And I, for one, would agree that anyone assenine enough to offer such a penile ad baculum should  be thunderbolted out of hus pontifical potty-chair as being less equipped to sit in it than the prosthetically-extended {Marianne}! )


What hidden fluctuations in value intuitions might a cross-gendering `thought experiment' uncover?

In Book I, the presentation of a female scientist pursued by a female terrorist left the readers of the 1960's utterly skeptical - but today, the characterizations appear less and less fantastic.

Try substituting three males for the three females; doesn't the plot now read more like some classic best-selling spy thriller?  Does the savage [War-relation] between the male protagonists seem quite as perverse as it does between [*Sarah] and [*Marianne]?

Now also contemplate the world of the harlot: don't brothel madams, obeying the orders of some background `Godfather', have a lot in common both with the {Marianne} of Book I and the {Marianne} of Book II?

Working on the hypothesis that the [War-relation] is not, has never been, genderbound, in Book II, by undertaking the explication of the gender-neutral religio-moral development of the child in the female modality, I was further able to shift the central theme of Book I (the economaterialist necessity of having to cut {[*Skeets]} adrift) to its analogue: the question of System-sanctioned `criminality' now recast in an entirely gender-free, culture-free, atemporal arena for the hardnosed depth-study of [*Classical `Humun Duty and Responsibility'].

Without this poetic exit to a new key, the unavoidably abrupt ending of Book I would have left the [Reader] aesthetically unsatisfied, for nothing was presented other than a statement of |brute fact|, empty of reflective content. For realistically there was nowhere left for Sarah to turn, no sane solution to the problem of `cutting Skeets adrift' except in the bitter temporary acceptance of an uncontrollable, [*Hellish(!)] state of affairs.

Upon completing Book I, [*I] must confess that I had verily painted myself into a corner!

Only with great effort did [The Author] force humself to take up the problem one more time, setting Book II on the broader, more generic canvas of postmodern "surrealist fiction"—so as to explore more closely the ideological schemata of world-historical classicoromantic thought (however muddled such *ersatz* Jungian archetypal constructs may ultimately be proven to be):

[*The Hero=*Sarah], impelled by the `life-boat ethic' of [War], again cuts down [*Skeets=*Hoffman] only at the expense of a long imprisonment inside the [Purgatory] of the vacant {Room with the Blue Door}.

Hus necessary act of [War] nevertheless costs hum hus original [*Identity] all the [*Beauty] of [*Sarah-Whole].

In this neoplatonic embodiment of [*The Laws] sits the promised Kingdom: a

a Hero's {Mun-made-Heaven}, sculpted from
                    [*Matter >Willed< into a *Beauty] by [mun-defining*Mun]}

Here, the muddled Zionist concept of [A People Who Are Chosen] is traded for the global Romantic posit of [We |The*People| Who Choose]

> {The Hero's escape from Purgatory} whether in the dream(?) or in the reality(?)) comes only through the existential priesthood of Citizenship (a solution that Socrates exemplified) in the Virtuous Soldier's return as the vigorous embodiment of [*The Laws]. ([The Mother] forced by the life-boat ethic of economic War to abort or abandon hus child, also suffers the same scar upon hus [*Personhood], but this parallel allegory is more often condemned than glorified in epic record.)

But it must be an aestheticomoral choice not to act with criminality if [Freedom] and [*Beauty] are to remain [*One], and emergent [Mun-Sarah] therefore to [*Become(!)]. (Compare this with Friedrich Schiller's aestheticomoral theory.) *Nota Bene* that only the already aestheticomorally `Law Abiding' are aestheticomorally compelled to obey `The Laws'!

I am loathe to interrupt my peripathesis with an impromptu digression on the "objective correlatives" that accompany this line of reasoning; however, in the event you may have failed to make note of it, the "harsh reality" of Sarah's world remains (intentionally!) unstated in the various alternate readings that may be given to Book II.

Consider the very likely "naturalistic" possibility that the |brute fact| was that Sarah really did go to the Cafeteria, just as Skeets had gone there, and had spoken up, and was taken away and was psychiatrically murdered. Then, after many shock treatments and months of rehabilitation, hu was returned, dumbly, complacently, even gratefully, to the parental arms of the Corporation, to "live happily ever after" teeing off at the Corporate Golf Course and splashing in the Secretarial Pool.

On this reading, Sarah's final, tragic, erroneous self-indictment of |The omssive sin of Silence| is the {Gothic Horror} of the Chronicles, the crime too terrible for Sarah to contemplate, and the world-historical "brute fact" of BOOK II: the |brute fact| that Sarah has no memory of hus own [*Heroism] but only of of hus final, imagined, irreparable, eternal, self-deprecating, unbearable [*Cowardice(!)].

Where then, in this "naturalistic" account of the matter, is [*Divine Justice] except in the self-healing {*Dream of [*Conscience]} that reconstructs for hum a new beginning, a renewed opportunity to achieve hus [*Moral Redemption]?
(But if there is no [*Gud] and no promised *Gudheaven/*Gudhell], *what* is there to guarantee our psychomoral `humun demand' that there be [*Justice]?)

With this kind of "objective correlative" pause for a moment then read all those passages again and ask yourself:

is the *Classical picture of [Mun], dominant even in modern religioexistentialist thought, really adequate?

For although *Classically we may forgive [*Gud] for not immediately avenging us, no promissory note given by [The State] carries the same line of credit. (Nor can purely economic reparations make up for it! - not even happy splashes in the Secretarial Pool!)  Such an existential void cannot even be filled through the age-old lie of Gudprosthesis:

what is required is a set of new parameters from which to view the concept of [*The Sanctity of The Self]

one which |This Poet| has the temerity to preview in the herein, and perhaps develop further in future work should I, thanks to modern science, live to be as old as Methuselah.

As a preliminary hypothesis, let me declare that I can see an epistemological strategy that will permit existential-deontological models to fill the psychomoral void in a manner more `synthetic a priori necessary' than that offered by the kind of discombobulated familial relationships which historicopolitically commit us to bogus jurisprudential strategies >versus-Cain< that have no positive effect >pro-Abel<.

For if [*Consciousness] is naturalistically ubiquitous, and [*Self] merely flotsam in the flow of the great river of {Awareness}, then [*Justice], [*Vengeance], [*Anger], [*Hatred], all appear as a smiting not of [Siblings] but of [*One's Own Face(!)].

The [War-relation] and its sociodarwinian implication of *sibling-vs-sibling* mellows down to one of peaceful [Compromise and Arbitration]  through the gentle intervention of mature and multivalued `Reasoning' between all the opposing parts of [*Self(!)].

Isn't [*Love of Self], [*Respect for Self] a much more spontaneous, natural place to begin than from a belabored >Gudordained<
[*Love of One's Enemy]?

In such a world, it is not an Avenging [*Gud] who holds us hostage:
[*We Hold Ourselves Hostage]

and that is a |brute fact| of ubiquitous [*Awareness(!)] that compells [Each*Awareness(!)] to mature toward `Individual Responsibility' from [*Birth] and [*Before] and [*Beyond].

Under this expanded concept of >Self<, [*Love of Self=The* Sacred] can be conserved interpersonally without the concept of >Gud< mediating it."

*Gud,* like *Phlogiston,* becomes an excessive ontological posit." (I credit my life-partner and early multimedia collaborator, Billie Taulman, with this penetrating observation first presented to me in 1954 as hus argument for our mutual embrace of a `Pious Atheism' as part of our public platform for human rights activism in the arts.)

For it is Sarah's [*Self-consciousness] as the |brute fact| of {Sarah}'s [*Being(!)] which both condemns and redeems |Absolutely|, *only when and only* *for as long as* {Sarah}=[*Sarah(!)].

Unlike its close cousins, `Pietism' and `Ethical Agnosticism', such a commitment to a `Pious Atheism' is predicated on the religiomoral working hypothesis that *all* Gud ontologies must be held to be [fundamentally sacrilegious(!)]}.  (On this covertly feminist position also hangs the spiritual future of the entire humun race and the humun rights of billions!)

There are, of course, other problems with this view which merit lengthy discussion elsewhere, but only after we have climbed out of the `picture' constructed in Book II.

Getting back to the other point I was making earlier:

> in contrast to Sarah, the [Aristocratic Marianne] seen as the embodiment of the powergroup within the extremist totalitarian [State] was fashioned to reflect the black-and-white thinking of the once fervently devout and now wholly disillusioned fascist/dialectical materialist.
>
> Marianne has what hu has through birth and power, and maintains it (even against hus own most gentle and noble inclinations) through a willful and bitter exercise of corrupt power.
>
> Hu defends hus choice strictly with pragmatic arguments;  hu knows hu is  morally wrong, but hu has chosen to be wrong on the grounds *that doing the right thing* would be [irresponsible] and that hus means are the only means the politicophysical economies permit.
>
> Marianne has chosen to remain in Hell until Justice has been done to All - and laughs even as hu burns, for hus `Moral Freedom' proceeds from a workaholic compulsion to |Perfection|, not from anything this world can offer.
>
> Marianne defies the world to bring hum to trial -- and, in the real world, hu has every legal reason (under the guise of military or police gudsanctions) to expect a full acquittal for most of hus political crimes, and immunity from prosecution for the rest of them through the general failure of [The System]
>
> Marianne is, after all, only following the orders that proceed from the higher authority of a rational body of political theory; hu is heroically waging a just war against an enemy that cannot be overcome except

through the unbridled exercise of Caesar's power.

Yet if and when Marianne finally decides to step out of [*Hell(!)], and return to a [*Classical Humun] identity, hu too will have to stand as Sarah, anxious to end hus exile, to march royally against humself. For the alternative would leave hum |something-less-than-Mun|. But Marianne has considered that possibility too:

> Hu has only contempt for the [Physical] therefore hus [Body] may be sacrificed to the cause of [Humun Progress] -- *insectlike*, hu is willing to allow both hus spiritual and physical |Self| to be treated as disposable, willing to bequeath hus [*Free Will] to [Mun*Sarah] or to the `clones' of [Marianne].

> Note also that hu has no physical fear of Hell's torments. It is only through hus as-yet-nonmanifest "Immortal Soul" that Marianne could be influenced. Only the prospect of a total, interplanetary/multiuniverse annihilation of the species would give hum pause. Why?

> > Because despite its emphasis on the individual, on private [*Conscience], the *Classical view of [Humun*Perfection] monistically envisions only [One*Gud], [One*Person], [One*Cosmic*Picture], [One Unified Science], etc. ( i.e., all "*Perfect" mun are alternate pictures of the same [*Mun"]).

> > Wherefore the whole species is the keeper of [*Marianne]'s "Immortal Soul", no matter how damned a >concrete< instance of >Marianne< may be.

Here then is the Romantic *Gestaldt* flypapering both {Sarah} and {Marianne} (and temporarily, most probably |The Author| and |The Reader| as well):

> Whether {Marianne} chooses, sanely, to abandon the goal of [*Wholeness], or chooses, romantically, to seek hus [Higher Self] makes little personal difference to hum - for hu has decided to postpone

[Salvation] and leave it to posterity.

And {Marianne} is morally justified in doing so, because >The System< has failed and hu is therefore not obligated to act morally.

Hus professed [Humun] love for [The Sacred] makes a difference to hum - not in the absurd and impossible `Afterlife', but in |the next generation| once [The System] has been restored to proper function.

(This, of course, is the materialist theory put forth repeatedly in neo-Brechtian "Gudfather" apologies for the sanctioned co-presence of organized crime as a genuine counter-culture and guerrilla Alterstate activity.)


Note that in such classical "individualist" moralities `Soul' must be seen as an excessive and subsidiary concept to that of [*Conscience]. And, most disturbingly, it also forms the basis for the proliferation of "satanic cult" Antistate constituencies, which parallel in reverse the very rituals of the ultra-stringent unworkable theories of the organized religions which give rise to them and which many in the congregation soon find they cannot live with. For such reasons, my abstract 'thought experiment' appears to me most relevant!

In such schemata, `Soul', loosely equivalent to [*I-am-Aware!], can reside wherever and however as (>I<or >Gud< ) please. But [*Conscience] must reside only in the [*Person] who alone is held accountable -- "operant conditioning" be damned!

Certainly for the scientist [*Conscience] is recognized as a necessary orthogonal function preserving sanity and personal integrity—an integrity socially created and socially conserved, but also psychologically essential to "rational" (i.e., "nonpathological" and "nonschizoid") `humun' behavior.

Yet the materialist's existentially modified >Conscience< can and often must bend opportunistically, through the structured intervention of >The System<, to permit selective >State+Gud-sanctioned< `criminal' acts ostensibly for the purpose of `group-survival'.

If most of the above seems too familiar, then all the better!

Now having painted my picture, framed it, and hung it on the wall, it is time for me to alienate myself from my own construction so as to better reflect on the bizarre consequences of this entrenched ideological paradigm.

As has been pointed out, the polisocmor question considered in Books I and II is the world-historical problem generated by `the lifeboat ethic'.

The [*Classical] solution is seen to come through the progressive refinement of humun institutions that eliminate conditions where it must be invoked, thereby increasing individual humun freedom of >normative< choice (while at the same time decreasing the number of opportunities for making truly unique and individual [concrete(!)] > not necessarily normative< value-judgments and hence ultimately, nevertheless still acting in behalf of `Group Mind' to depress [*Authentic(!) Self-consciousness].

|The Author's| difficulty with the above arises from an adherence to this timeworn and thus-far bankrupt problem-solving matrix:

i. in contemplating the quasi-utopian case, where most humun conflict has been reduced to trivial family squabbles and small-town storms in a teacup, and the only thing to look forward to is a sleepy retirement to an idyllic green pasture that depresses existential awareness of distinctly [Humun*Being]. (Not that a smattering of such islands of tranquility isn't always welcome!)

ii. on trying on scifi alternatives for future `Mun', |The Author| keeps running into clones of [Marianne] or into [Mothra] and [Max Headroom].

iii. on trying to act `Humunly' within the present existentially-cataclysmic environment, [*The Author], like all social worker classes, finds humself inundated and nearly drowned by life-boat-ethic' situations arising out of public apathy in >The State< generated by the renegade fluctuation of the concept of >Mun/mun<

iv. on trying to find the source of such public apathy, |The Author|

stumbles on the problem of do-gooder "burn out" which seems to be affecting everyone.

v.  while most of such "burn out" is probably really due to economic stress, viruses and pollution, the old-fashioned vaccine which once seemed to have a special ability to motivate change—the ideological vaccine of "|The Sacred|" — is either being misused or trashed.

vi.  this prompts [The Author] to challenge the *Classical ideal of the ["workable utopian" State] by asking some unbiased and pointed questions:

What, ultimately, is Mun?  A monkey?  An insect?

Is there anything [*Sacred(!)] or [Real(!) in the material universe that remains intact even in utopian environments where moral consciousness, through ritual, lies dormant?

If we give in to humunitarian "burn out" and eliminate billions of [Skeets] so that |We the Strong| can immediately achieve and enjoy our new mun-made *Paradise*, will we still, like {Sarah}, need to keep biting the *Apple* in order to remain [*Humun]?

From a cosmologist's standpoint, no Survivalist's monstrous "final solution" can be categorically rejected on moral grounds until metaphysical questions about the nature of spatiotemporal reality, as defined by the  physicist and the information scientist, are satisfactorily resolved.

Scientists evade such moral dilemmas by waiting for some prophecied "New Messiah" to arrive from the religions or the humanities to interpret the progress of the physical sciences within the languages of science.  But this is a hypocritical epistemic strategy that inevitably traps us into either the [Altermun-Marianne]'s or the [Antimun-Marianne]'s programmes of "humun-garbage-disposal" often euphemized and/or legitimized as [Social Darwinism].

Scientists should be able to study both `Religion' and `Morals' without reducing either category to Munlogy(Anthropology) or Psychology or Sociology, and should be able, under a systematic Religious Science, and a systematic Moral Moral Science, to come up with fruitful ontological hypotheses contiguous with the epistemic objectives of a unified science. (And I don't mean an ontology of quarks and muons!  Real `Courage&Conscience' are lacking.)

Only when we can arrive at a formal nondarwinian explication of a new concept of [The* Sacred] contiguous with the theoretical foundations of science shall we be able to resolve questions dealing with `the lifeboat ethic' taken out of their multicultural classicoreligious contexts, to arrive at a global unisci [Meta-Theory of Mun].

This is the same larger question still left unresolved in Book II.

Let us therefore restate it:

> Can one arrive at a universally valid moral theory that will take into account humun evolution beyond the species level?

> Or is {mun-defined Mun}(i.e., the hybrid {Sarah/Marianne}) doomed to perpetual >Dybbukian< transformations—doomed to perpetual war, and system-sanctioned criminality, or— what may be even worse from a world-historical view—doomed to ruminate, after the `Survivalist holocaust', like contented cattle in islands of `utopian tranquility'?

> What, if ~[Gud] defines a distinctly [*Humun] existence?

> And if a pupal-stage humunity finally emerges from its earthly cocoon into one or more extrabiological forms of being within the intergalactic universe, which distinctly [Humun] features will ultimately survive such long-distance permutations?

While it may not at first be obvious, the above is subtly equivalent to the following:

> |What shall be the nature and persona of [Mun-created-Gud]|?

That is, because from a realistic and world-historical standpoint, {Gud} did not create either {Mun} or {mun}; rather, [mun] created [*Gud].

And this muncentric act, in which a {Gud} was created in the image either of *Adam or of *Christ, prompts an even more radical inquiry:

> Is {Gud}, like {The State}, authentically only one more "prosthetic extension" of mun?

And if so, then why |Gud|, why not |Supermun|?

In our final encounter with Marianne in Book II, this is the inevitable outcome of the classicoromantic `Supermun' programme. And the world-historical temptation toward the evolutionary achievement of [Mun-Gudhood] for either Sarah or Marianne is not seen as heresy but as the legitimate legacy of any classico-religious doctrine that preaches a {Parent:Child} image-equivalence between {Gud} and {Mun}.

The inadequacy of this picture increases, not diminishes, whenever  mun-defined >Mun< acquires, through science, the ability to see the world from mun-defined/Humun-defined {Gud's Eye}; for two nagging questions still remain unanswered, perhaps for all `Eternity'—questions which, if unanswered by a satisfactory [*Supermun], condemn all three of my characters to an ever-diminishing concept of |Mun|, i.e.,

> (a) What is the nature (or meaning) of "The Real"?

> (b) Is [The*Sacred] ever [Real(!)] in a |Random| Universe?

But abandon that classicoromantic picture and a whole new strategy appears: for it is my sincere contention that, for all common characterizations of (a) above, (b) can be answered intelligibly and nonparadoxically in the affirmative—if we reject all ontological posits of [Gud].

As I have previously noted, *Gud*, like *Phlogiston*, is ontologically dispensable in favor of the concept of [Scientific*Truth]—a [Scientific*Truth] which, for a [Self=The Sacred], provides the only means of egress for a cosmic [*Awareness] which cannot escape the |brute fact| of the |Humun Condition| even unto the outermost rim of the Universe—an [*Awareness] that is fated to return, *Big Bang* after *Big Bang*, to an internal [*Hell(!)] of its Own Making until such time as it can congeal itself into a harmonic [*Wholeness]—a [*Flowering of Being].

> If this posit continues to startle you, just ask yourself what, in your deepest {Self}, you value more—what would you, with your |Whole Self-Conscious Being| be willing to endure the worst of all deaths for—the [*Love(!)] of {Gud} or the [*Love(!)] of {Truth}?

If there were some means of persuading you that you couldn't have both, would you indeed prefer {Gud}?   The intellectually honest among us would have to admit that >Truth< —no matter how arcane and elusive the concept may be—is both more "logically primitive" and (hence) more [*Sacred(!)]".

Nor can there be any theologian's escape from this intuition in the smug assurance that [Gud] and [Truth] are |One|; for [Gud] is an ontological posit, and >Truth< is not an `object' but a `value' assigned to logico-theoretical constructions, and |Gud=T| is an identity relation between an `object' and a `truth-value' that, if metalinguistically posited as [*True(!)], merely begs the question!

This new start from a cosmic [Awareness] that postulates [The Self=The Sacred] ought to do for Moral Science what Relativity did for Physics.

Grounding `The Sacred' in the `Self' wherever |Self-Consciousness| emerges, forces the Moral Observer to become the center of the Universe, no longer alienated from an `Other' which does all the actual *Willing, *Creating, *Knowing, and so on, from some vague and arbitrary parameter set *ever beyond language*.

It preserves the real sense of the concept of `Freedom and Responsibility' for `All Mun', transforms `All Mun' into |Shepherds| rather than |Sheep|, connects `Each Mun' to the common bond of [*Selfhood-in-Awareness].

It further `Self-mandates' an `enlightened Self-Interest' —a cosmic evangelism toward a concrete goal of |Humun Progress| for [All Conscious Beings], whether these be {Biological} or {Whatever}, [*Who] share in the |brute fact| and >Truth< of the |Humun Condition|.

This kind of `Self' is `Recurrent', `Inescapable', 'Communal', giving new sense and orientation to the biblical dictum: *"Whatsoever Ye Do Unto Each Other, Ye Do Also Unto Me"* and spontaneous endorsement to the christian maxim,

*"Do unto others as you would have them do unto you."*

Are you happy with this new picture?

It may yet prove be the most savage and dreadful of all(!), but it does provide an escape from macrocosmic ennui and daily routine, and the dull prospect of ending our zillion millennia as nothing more than contented cows and couch potatoes! For under this view we do simultaneously sit, eternally and recurrently (insofar as those terms make biological sense), in both a `Heaven' and `Hell' of `Our Own Making', wherein *Equity, *Justice, Humun*Purpose, Humun*Entelechy, are all >Self-determined< and therefore [*Free(!)].

But what about [*Love] as viewed from this Muncentric set of parameters?

[Self*Love] sounds dreadfully dull, even masturbatory!

Does this new view condemn us to an inescapable homo-eroticism, a `narcissism' of cosmic breadth?

Are all of [My*Embraces] [Self*Embraces]? (NOTA BENE that I have entirely wiped out {Gender} from this semantic!)

No! In a cosmology allowing for >extensional truth< there is an [*Other] in our universe which is [*Other-than-Observers] and it is that inescapable presence, that alienating |brute fact| delimiting, partitioning, grounding each minute instant of [My*Self-Conscious*Being], which is—howbeit ever savage, impersonal and uncaring—both [*My Lover] and [My Beloved] and heteroerotic genome to [*All My Clones]!

But >Truth<, mind you, is not a [*Person].
Nor is it in itself an [*Object] in any ordinary sense of the word.  In all instances of our experimental interaction with the [Other] beyond language, it is simply a |Feedback(!)|, a |Signal(!)| a [*YES(!)].)

But I swear to you that although, like Sarah, I too have always been demanding "carnal knowledge of an |Angel|, I did not begin my present project with any such startling conclusions in mind!
I was only intent upon constructing a model that would effectively sort out all the confusion in my thought.
I simply assumed that my deep-rooted personal hostility to the male-defined concept of {Gud} was politico-psychologically oppressive and contemptuous.  The `thought experiment' of Book II was specifically devised  to untether my thought in order to ferret out the gender-free image of [Mun] from the lesser (and polihisto-contaminated) image of {Man}.
I hoped through such a mental honing to adumbrate the reasons for my gut-objection to all "God" posits as being not merely impure because sexist, but because the theological-ontological assertion—even in its most refined and nonsexist formulation—is fundamentally excessive, schizoid and prone to pathological contamination;  more often than not homoerotic,  lascivious, narcissistic and idolatrous;  psychologically and epistemically obstructive; further, entirely eliminable in favor of a `Social-Conscience-driven' morally-responsible characterization of [The Ideal State]; and, at least to |The Author|, intuitively also *[sacrilegious(!)].
But the epistemological necessity of categorically rejecting the entire Gud-paradigm was not obvious to |me| when, as both female and feminist, I attempted to contemplate [*God] in its male-related image.
As gender-bound female I had always been far too prone to dismiss my personal objection to the male-related image of either {Gud} or {Supermun} as an extension of my existential rejection of the psychosexual image of
{The Male=Object-of-Religious*Worship}
as {symbol-of-political-subjugator-and-molestor}.

And it was only after first constructing, then deconstructing {Supermun/Marianne} in the light of my information science model of [*Consciousness(!)] that I finally found my way out of the picture.

But after contemplating the truly abominable, spiritual invasiveness of Supermun/Marianne as it is felt by [Mun*Sarah] - a generic `rape-relation' of [mun-on-*Mun] - such psycho-political oppression, such spiritual invasion, really has nothing to do with the [Gender] of the protagonists, now, does it?

It is the {Gudpicture} - the entire {Gudparadigm}
that offends and oppresses [*Me].

But enough said for one sitting!

If |You| are still with |Me|, if by now I have not thoroughly befuddled |You|, then by all means interface with |Me| again in my forthcoming offerings wherein I promise to reveal to |You|, insofar as my own poetic sight is |Gospel| the full and unequivocal meaning of |The*Sacred|.

*ArtemisSmith* 1989

## 2015 ADDENDUM:

When this was first published, some of my colleagues including R.E.L Masters and wife Jean Houston were both kind enough to read SKEETS in its entirety and to separately comment on it. By 1989, most of my esteemed academic mentors had long-since passed on. Masters' published review, as renowned phenomenologist and sexologist, confined itself to BOOKS I&II. Houston, as renowned philosopher of religion and cultural anthropologist, hit upon the key difficulty in BOOK III: *What do I mean when referring to the |Other| beyond language*, and this prompted me to add/correct the passage

But >Truth<, mind you, is not a [*Person].
Nor is it in itself an [*Object] in any ordinary sense of the word. In all instances of our experimental interaction with the [Other] beyond language, it is simply a |Feedback(!)|, a |Signal(!)| a [*YES(!)].)

156

to subsequent editions of BOOK III.  I very much thank her for her guidance.

Obviously the presence of an external [*YES(!)] is the mystical element in all our search.  Since the many [natural languages] of Mathematics form the most primitive foundations for all our thought [c.f. Russell, Wittgenstein, Quine], beyond which no other "language" exists, and Mathematics is not free of paradox, the extensional [*YES(!)] underlying the semantic of our thought is paradoxical.  With paradox comes the {Freedom to say *[NO(!)}.

Under some rule, {*Anything*} may be possible!

*ArtemisSmith* 2015

ArtemisSmith's

GLBT Science Fiction Classic

The SKEETS Diptych

Testament of Sarah

Flowers of Marianne

the savant garde workshop

SAG HARBOR, NEW YORK, USA

# MIRACULOUS Sacred Heart ATHEIST PRAYER ICON

Billionaires, stop asking Congress to raise your taxes and simply take matters into your own hands!  Make the Miracles our Society needs.  Maverick it like all true Saints have always done! Take the initiative, empty your pockets of all that spare change and help us help the homeless and the politically and economically displaced.  And, while you are at it,

BUY THIS MAGNIFICENT antique lemon, SPEND SOME MORE BUCKS RESEARCHING AND AUTHENTICATING IT, THEN DONATE IT BACK TO US AND MAKE YOURSELF BIG POCKET-CHANGE ON THE RESALE AND/OR THE WRITE-OFF of this Atheist-Anointed 6"x 8" miraculous ArtemisSmith collectible

## Probably Late 18th or Early 19th Century Oil-on-Panel

Perhaps a hands-on Curatorial Copy of a lost c.1450 Original Old Master? Note the strange etched encryptions on the halo surrounding the figure - was someone anxious to preserve a hidden Da Vinci code?

This unsigned magnificently-executed oil-on-panel prayer icon could easily pass for an authentic Leonardo, but two expert auctioneer appraisers have evaluated it as having less than a $100 market value - this, despite its age, vintage framing, and master workmanship!  Whoever copied this must have had an excellent original to work from!  However, "There's no market for religious art,"  both appraisers said, "Sorry!"

*Well, confirmed mystical atheist Annselm ArtemisSmith Morpurgo thinks otherwise!*
"This was the first person I fell in love with as a child," she writes. "Too bad for the beard, the painting should have been Unisex and Unirace, because it isn't the face we love or pray to, but the whole concept of Universal Love that speaks through it.  A great artist who deeply felt that Love must have painted the Original, and that makes this well-crafted Copy a magnificent preservation, and perhaps the only remaining record, of a lost masterpiece!"
ArtemisSmith continues: "Just because it has a sectarian theme shouldn't turn us away from its hidden mystical meaning.  It is possible to be an Atheist and still believe that there is something greater than ourselves sitting out there, waiting for us to recognize our unlimited potential to become *Masters of the Universe* through Love and Understanding.  Forget all the mythical crap that the merchants of religious garbage are feeding the masses!  True Love and Compassion dwelling in each for each other is all anyone needs to preserve our identity as uniquely Human.
And that is the Source of all Miracles!"

The Observer is the Center of the Universe

The Observer does Logic and Mathematics *(which are the languages of Thought)*.

All Thought is Linguistic (and therefore Intersubjectively Communicative).

All Human Experience is Linguistic *('scientific truth' is therefore necessarily grounded in |The Intersubjective Observer|)*

All Language is Socially Relative

Logic has been shown to be merely one suburb of Mathematics.

Mathematics has been shown to be an imperfect and open system.

Mathematics tolerates and 'negotiates' Paradox *(by taking advantage of internal inconsistencies such as the existence of irrational numbers)*.

This negates the possibility of **Concrete Perfection** and
opens up the **Descriptive Multiverse**

|Mathematical Language| existentially notates the **'ergodic stuff'** of Chaos            and encompasses **'all that can be spoken**.

Beyond **'All that can be spoken'** is Logically-Necessary Silence

**'All that can be spoken'** is both social and quantifiable *(including the reflection of Individual Mind upon Itself which is |Self-Consciousness|)*.

> **System Architecture** may limit **Present Form**
> but it is not to be confused with **Spirit**
> which is **Self-Conscious Identity-through-Change**
> or with **Soul**
> which is the **Timeless Moral Quality of Spirit as Formally Unique**

|Individual Identity| is comprised of both **Spirit** and **Soul**
and rests upon growing social values and relations
and persists in hyperspace
and can shape-shift beyond **Initial System Architecture**

## The immediate socio-political implications of this view are that

1. **Gender** is accidental and irrelevant to **Spirit** or **Soul**
2. **Human Identity** can shape-shift beyond the **Biological**
3. **Soul** has **Descriptive Perfection** but not **Existence**

*Artemis Smith* **1972**

CATEGORIES: BIOGRAPHY:
FEMINIST, LGBT, AND HISTORY

# artemis smith

holocaust refugee,
multinational poet,
novelist, playwright,
human rights activist,
futurist and philosopher
of science

check rare book listings at:
amazon.com
borders.com
shop.barnesandnoble.com
www.ArtemisSmith.com

(Born:
Baroness Annaselma
Larsen-Nilsen-Vinga
Morpurgo in Rome,
Italy, 1934.)

download some of the
key works of this
underground multimedia
poet and philosopher
who was blacklisted
for four decades for
her early activism in
defense of feminism
and integrationism.

**alive and well
and producing in
The Hamptons, USA**

an architect of the
human rights movements of the
1950's and '60's

coined and
stylized
the 1950's
Unisex and Unirace
Movements

**1949
founded the
Savant Garde Movement
and its ethic of
inclusion**

opposed the 1960's
and 70's drug culture takeover
of the avant garde arts

**1965
gave the first
history making
'Come out of the Closet'
speech to the
gay activist community**

**1966 - 1973**
authored the first explanatory model
of human consciousness contiguous
with the languages of information science

**1973 - 1976**
sued a major segment of
the academic-industrial
complex to accelerate
affirmative action

**1982 - 1988**
developed
published and produced
the first computer desk-top
on-demand novels

the
savant garde workshop
sag harbor . new york . usa ™
1-878998-30-7

Futurist Philosopher Annselm L.N.V. Morpurgo, M.A., CPC
also known in the Arts as ArtemisSmith
1934 …..………… ?

www.ingramcontent.com/pod-product-compliance
Lightning Source LLC
Chambersburg PA
CBHW051617030426
42334CB00030B/3227